Roommates

Also by Max Apple

The Propheteers
The Oranging of America and Other Stories
Zip
Free Agents

Roommates

My Grandfather's Story

MAX APPLE

WARNER BOOKS

A Time Warner Company

243 4653

Special thanks to Terry Munisteri for her typing and encouragement and to Talya Fishman for everything.

Copyright © 1994 by Yom Tov Sheyni, Inc.
All rights reserved.

Warner Books, Inc., 1271 Avenue of the Americas, New York, NY 10020

A Time Warner Company

Printed in the United States of America

First Printing: June 1994

10 9 8 7 6 5 4 3 2 1

Library of Congress Cataloging-in-Publication Data

Apple, Max.
   Roommates : my grandfather's story / Max Apple.
     p.   cm.
   ISBN 0-446-51826-3
   1. Apple, Max—Family.   2. Authors, American—20th century—
Biography.   3. Grandfathers—United States—Fiction.   I. Title.
PS3551.P56Z47   1994
813'.54—dc20
[B]   93-45371
                                             CIP

Book design by H. Roberts

For Rocky's other grandchildren,
my sisters,
Bailey & Maxine

Roommates

Chapter 1

I had come to nominate a president; so had seven or eight hundred other hippies, yippies, pacifists, Black Panthers, macrobiotics, and assorted nonbelievers in the two-party system.

It was 1968. There were already one hundred thousand troops in Vietnam and more on the way. Inside, on the grass of the Michigan Union, Lyndon Johnson hung in effigy. On the stage of the second-floor ballroom where Eldridge Cleaver spoke about peace, his Black Panther bodyguards pointed machine guns toward the audience. Every time there was applause I started to duck.

Three other candidates waited to address the audience, but the crowd was in Cleaver's hands.

"Are you a faster?" someone asked me.

She wore a black T-shirt with a picture of Jimi Hendrix. Her sunglasses hung by a single temple post from a string around her neck. She was barefoot, and her blue jeans had a few tears around the knee. Her eyes were a little bloodshot.

If I had seen her on the street, I wouldn't have been surprised if she'd asked me for spare change. I would have given, and I would have remembered her.

"What's a faster?" I asked.

"If you don't know," she said, "then you're not one."

She looked at Cleaver, I looked at her.

"If you're just going to stare," she said, "I'll be happy to let you hold my driver's license photograph." She started to reach into the nylon waistpack that she wore at her belt.

"No picture," I said, "I prefer the real thing."

"Well, the real thing is a lot messier."

"I'll take my chances," I said.

"Suit yourself," she said.

I followed her out of the ballroom. In the hallway there were at least twenty tables filled with propaganda leaflets. She stopped to pick up a picture of a napalmed child and then a pamphlet from the macrobiotic table.

"Why are you following me?" she asked.

"I'm not following," I said. "I came to get a pamphlet, too. You're not the only one interested in macrobiotics. I'd like some more information."

"Ask one of those guys." She motioned toward two young men in sunglasses who stood behind the table. Then she slipped back into the crowd and headed toward the staircase.

I pushed a shirtless delegate with a peace symbol tattooed on his shoulder out of my way to catch up with her. "Hold on," I said. "Don't run away. We've just met."

"I'm sorry," she said, "but I'm busy. Not just the convention. Personal stuff. I'll see you around."

She walked quickly down the big marble stairs, and again I followed. She noticed me at the first landing.

"Hey," she said, "you're getting to be a pain in the ass."

"If you'd stop running away from me, I wouldn't have to follow you."

"Okay," she said. "What do you want?"

We were standing in the main lobby of the Student Union, beneath a big bronze chandelier.

I introduced myself, so did she.

"I can't really stop to talk," she said. "I'm in a hurry."

"I'm not," I said. "Can I come along?"

We walked down University Avenue. She stopped at a yellow Plymouth convertible. The backseat was full of clothes and boxes. An uncovered pillow lay on top. Although we hadn't said another word, we both understood that I was going along. She leaned over to unlock the passenger door.

"I hate to be so obvious again," I said, "but do you always carry so many changes of clothes?"

"I've been looking for a place for my stuff for two weeks. It's no problem to find a place to crash somewhere for a night, but if they give you a closet, suddenly they want you to sign a lease. It's like clothes and records are more important than people."

She turned up Hill Street, lined on both sides with sororities, fraternities, and large houses that the university owned. Only one building stood out among those early-twentieth-century mansions that now housed Greeks and institutes. She parked in front of the multicolored three-story Victorian headquarters of the Rainbow People's party.

"I'll see if I can store my stuff here. It's my last hope."

She closed the car door, walked toward the house. I watched her reach the purple steps. Then she stopped and turned back. She opened the passenger door and squatted so she could look me in the eye.

"You can sit here if you want, but I might be a while."

"It's okay," I said. "I'll be a security guard for your stuff."

"I'd invite you in, but you never know what's going on in there, and I'll have to see if there's a spot for all this."

"Would it be safer there than in the car?"

"Probably not," she said, "but what's ever safe? It's just an illusion. I think you should go. If I had a phone I'd give you the number."

"No, I'll wait."

She stood up. "When you do get tired and decide to leave, please keep your finger on the button so the door will stay locked." She lowered her dark eyes. I had the feeling that she really didn't want me to leave no matter what she said.

"It's a guy I'm going to see in there. That's why I can't take you inside. It would spoil any chance I have." She closed the door and ran toward the house.

I rolled down the window. Mentioning the guy had done it. Jealousy made me decide to risk it.

"I've got a closet," I called out, "with a sliding door and two shelves. It's yours if you want it."

"Why didn't you say so," she said. She ran back to the car even faster than she'd hurried away.

In the car she was excited but a little suspicious. "Are you holding out while you decide how much rent to charge?"

"I hadn't even thought of that."

"Then do it now, because I don't want to carry all the stuff up and then have you say it's two hundred a month or something."

"No charge," I said.

"You're sure?"

"Positive."

"One other thing," she said. "I want you to get this straight up front. It's just the clothes and the records and the books and the shoes."

"That's plenty for one closet," I said.

"I mean, it's just the stuff—not me."

I asked her to speak softly when I unlocked the door. It took us only two trips from the car. Her clothes and books stacked neatly on the floor required less room than I thought. She didn't have much.

"Let's put it in the closet," she said.

"It's a mess now," I said. "Leave it here. I'll put everything away in the morning."

"Let's do it now and I'll help—I don't want to stick you with all that work."

"Tomorrow," I said, trying to be as firm as I could without scaring her away.

She looked around the apartment, the two stuffed chairs, the wooden dinette table, the wall-to-wall carpeting. "This doesn't feel like a student apartment," she said.

I pulled out my wallet and showed her my ID.

"That's not what I mean—the place is so clean—you've got a real living room—there's not even any stains on the carpet."

I turned on the TV to divert her. The ten o'clock news was already over. She plopped down next to me. The weather and sports were on when I put my arm around her.

"How come you live so far from campus?" she said. "I'll bet for what you're paying out here you could be on State or East University and roll out of bed right before class."

I thought I heard something, so I didn't answer. I was thinking about how I'd explain the stacks of books and clothes.

"You sure you don't want me just to go?" she said.

I must have been quiet and straining to listen longer than I realized. She started to move away.

"No," I said. "Please stay. We'll watch the late movie."

"You're sure?"

"I'm sure."

I was thinking about what she told me—the ground rules, just the clothes, not her; but when I put my lips right in front of hers she didn't resist.

When I looked up John Wayne was shooting at someone on my black-and-white Philco portable. I wouldn't have looked up so soon, but this time I did hear a noise.

I heard footsteps. A door closed, and then the toilet flushed.

I sat up quickly and moved away from her. She didn't seem surprised at all.

"Your roommate?" she asked.

I hadn't said anything about a roommate.

"Yeah," I said. "That's why I wanted to be quiet and not put your stuff in the closet tonight."

"Why didn't you just say so?"

"I didn't want you to change your mind about leaving your things here."

"Change my mind—are you kidding? If not for you, my next stop would probably be the Salvation Army."

She moved close to me again—but I was no longer comfortable.

"You want something to eat?" I asked. I stood up and tiptoed to the kitchen.

"Do I have bad breath?" she whispered.

"No," I whispered back, "I just don't want to wake my roommate."

"Do I kiss that loud?"

I came back to the couch and kissed her again.

"Yes," I said, "much too loud."

"Maybe it's you," she said.

"Can't be," I said. "I practice silence all the time." That was the truth.

"Is your roommate one of those guys who pulls all-nighters and then sleeps for a year?"

"No," I said, then I kissed her again just to keep from talking.

We were as silent as could be—she even opened her eyes, tapped my shoulder, and put her forefinger to our mutual lips, then asked me with her eyes if she was being quiet enough.

I nodded, and she was quiet. We both were—even John Wayne on the screen had his volume so low that you only knew a shot had been fired when someone hit the ground.

From the bedroom we heard a high-pitched wheeze, followed by a fluffy noise of flesh—as if the lips were clapping hands.

We both opened our eyes but stayed in a kiss. There was another wheeze and clap of the lips and then the phrase "son of a bitch" in a powerful grunting whisper.

She laughed. I stood up and started moving her clothes to the other side of the couch, nearer the window, where maybe they wouldn't be so obvious to someone who might emerge from the bedroom behind us.

It was a mistake. I carried a stack of books supporting the top one with my chin, and a slippery Modern Library edition of *The Rise and Fall of the Roman Empire* fell. As I reached for it—the whole stack hit the carpet. She tried to catch them and fell off the couch. That's where we were when my roommate ran in from the bedroom. Her clothes were spread around her, and she lay among a pile of her books. I stood looking at the mess I had created.

She and my roommate eyed one another. She waited a bit, then extended her hand. She was surprised but tried to act as if meeting an old man in long underwear could happen to anyone.

"Hi, I'm Debby," she said. "I'm sorry we woke you, it was an accident."

His blue eyes showed no hint of tiredness. He had snow white hair, was five feet tall, and weighed 110 pounds. He attacked.

"Ger out from here," he said. He rushed past both of us to grab an armful of clothes. As he carried them to the door we could see through the open snap of his union suit. Debby suppressed a laugh. I hurried to the hallway to pick up her clothes, but he had already tossed out another armful.

"I get the message," she said. "I can take the stuff out myself if you'll give me five minutes."

"Now," he said.

I met him at the door and caught the next load before he could throw her blouses into the hallway.

At my best I could have teased him or made up his kind of story: she had come to collect clothing for Jewish orphans or was a homeless waif thrown into the streets by his enemies, like Lyndon Johnson and Herbert Hoover. But I wasn't in the mood for teasing. Debby had picked up as much as she could carry and was at the door.

"Ger out," he grunted again.

"I'm gerring," she said, meeting his fierce look with one of her own. While they stared each other down I was in the hallway picking up shoes and shirts.

She grabbed them out of my arms, and some fell. I gathered them up and followed her outside. She was fighting back tears when I stopped her at the wheel of her convertible.

"I should have warned you," I said. "It's my fault."

"Will you bring the rest out?" she asked. "I don't want to see him again."

"I can explain. . . . Leave everything, tomorrow I'll put it in the closet."

"Please," she said, "I wanna get out of here."

I didn't have to go into the apartment, her things were all in the hallway. I reloaded her backseat.

She blew her nose and regained her composure.

"He's not always like this," I said.

"Even if he's paying more than half the rent," she said, "you're getting a bad deal."

Chapter 2

*T*hat roommate who chased Debby out of our apartment had been looking out for me all my life—maybe longer. Our bond began, I think, in January 1936, five years before my birth when my grampa Rocky, his son Max, two female cousins, and his son-in-law, Sam, who was my father, were in Max's black Chevrolet returning to Grand Rapids, Michigan, from a family wedding in Detroit.

It was about nine P.M., and Max was at the wheel. He was twenty-three and not too experienced at highway speeds, but his car was new and he enjoyed driving. He wasn't going too fast—he couldn't. The wind blew blinding snow at the car, and beneath the snow lay the dangerous black ice of Michigan winters.

Somewhere near Lansing, the Chevy skidded on one of those ice sheets and began to cross the median. Max hit the brake, the car spun off the road into a healthy elm tree.

The passengers were all thrown from the car. The steering wheel kept Max inside, but the pointed Chevrolet insignia penetrated his chest.

When the first ambulance arrived, the driver and the attendant left the two women where they were. They had been killed instantly. Rocky and my father were battered but conscious. They watched the two medical workers load Max onto a stretcher.

The ambulance, because of the treacherous weather, had to travel far slower than usual. The emergency medic put oxygen over Max's mouth and held a stethoscope to his heart. A few minutes from the hospital he removed the oxygen. "I'm sorry," he told Rocky, "he died." Rocky pushed open the door of the ambulance and tried to jump out. The medic and my father barely kept him from doing so.

Rocky never told me that story, never mentioned his son at all. What I know of my uncle Max comes from my grandmother, who never stopped mourning him, and from my mother, who even years later during my childhood still visited the cemetery so regularly that tombstones with Hebrew lettering are my earliest memories.

In many families there is a single defining event that changes everything. This was ours. Five years later, at my birth, my parents, grandparents, and my two sisters were all living together—a band of survivors. My arrival, I think, finally turned them toward forgetting. No one could replace their loss, but I entered the world loaded—they named me Max, and everyone had an equal share in me. I was born two generations deep.

In a big gray clapboard house in the industrial district of Grand Rapids my family began, like many immigrants, to put all they had into their children. In our case the grandchildren were the children as well.

At home we spoke Yiddish, but at school my sisters and I hung on to English like the life raft it was. Once we had the language we polished it. The girls become paragons of fluency, high school debate champs. They brought home gilded trophies that thrilled us.

Around the kitchen table it was the nineteenth century. In Yiddish the adults talked about the czar and pogroms—but in the dining room only the issues of the day passed my sisters' lips as they practiced debate before a large gilded mirror.

They quoted from *Time* and *Newsweek* and kept all the old magazines in stacks under their beds. My mother almost swooned when she looked up from washing dishes or cooking to see her debating daughters gesturing with their arms and using big words. My grandma thought their padded bras were a clever way to keep warm. My father carried their trophies in his truck to show them to the purchasing agents and plant managers in northern Michigan who sold him scrap steel and metal.

"You'll be a speaker, too," my mother promised me, but I didn't think so. I gravitated instead to an older set of debaters who didn't say "Excuse me" or interrupt in allotted two- or three-minute bursts. These debaters, Rocky and my grandma, weren't practicing, either. They wished upon one another cholera and ague and what they had, a life in exile among the goyim. If anyone gave out trophies for Yiddish cursing, they would have been daily winners.

Gootie, my grandma, was a short, large-boned woman who made the kitchen her kingdom. She entered the living room only on special occasions—like Monday night to watch "I Love Lucy." She had to think about her movements ever since she fell from a freight train in Russia during the First World War. Her broken leg, never properly set, left her dragging a stiff limb for the rest of her days. The disability made it necessary to plan her movements in advance. She did the same thing psychologically. Slow and careful in everything, she was the exact opposite of her speedy husband. They were the marriage of thought and action, and in constant conflict.

Rocky was a whirlwind and the family pioneer. He came to America on his own in 1914 and began immediately to work sixteen-hour days so he could bring his wife and two children, Bashy and Max, to Michigan. During what he called "the first war," none of his letters were answered. He didn't know where his family was or even if they were alive. But he saved his money and he kept writing.

After the war, when Gootie, my mother, and Max returned to their village from the big city of Odessa where the Russian government had shipped them, their house was a ruin and their German and Lithuanian paper money worthless. A few letters were waiting for them.

In Michigan Rocky went to night school, where he learned to read and write English. The only thing he did at less than top speed was sign his name. When he had to do so, usually on some kind of official form, he did it the way a good basketball player shoots free throws: he concentrated on mechanics. He braced himself with his left hand on the writing surface, checked the position of his thumb and forefinger on the pencil or ballpoint, and then executed the curves of "Herman," the slightly ridiculous American name that an immigration clerk gave him because "Yerachmiel" was too hard. The men who worked beside him at the American Bakery were smarter. When they couldn't say Yerachmiel, they called him Rocky, the name that stuck.

I never missed an opportunity to watch him sign "Herman." It was regal. He should have used a quill and a blotter. He always gave it a quick double check before he put the pen down. When I learned cursive in fourth grade I filled Palmer method notebooks practicing writing between the big lines and small lines with my name and his. Max Apple never got beyond a scrawl, but I could do "Herman Goodstein" like a master forger.

Gootie never learned English. That lack kept her housebound more than her lame leg did, but she made immobility a strength. She liked the rest of the family to report our experiences to her, and she rewarded us with her ironic commentaries on what we told her. A coffee cup always in front of her, her bad leg propped on a stool, she made her spot at the kitchen table the center of the household. She analyzed things and passed judgments. She kept a big white rag beside her to blow her nose and to wipe her eyes, which regularly leaked tears of laughter. She had two big things to laugh at—America and her husband.

What she knew about America she learned from looking at pictures in the newspaper, watching people on the street, or picking up the news and gossip that the family brought to her. Her longest field trips were our walks to the supermarket. She liked to go with me because I had the patience to read labels and explain what was in the cans and packets that were new and usually amusing to her.

I could read by five and liked to show off. We were quite a pair in the supermarket. I read the labels aloud in Yiddish, then together we tried to translate subtleties—things like the difference between tomato paste and tomato sauce. We spent a lot of time on such matters at the neighborhood A&P, while all around us gentiles roamed, loading their carts with what we knew were slabs of pork and shotgun shells.

We didn't go to the A&P to buy—my parents did that once a week in our dark green Pontiac—Gootie and I went to the store for entertainment. The aisles of the A&P were our movies. She liked to watch people load up on absurdities like tissues and deodorant. She could look at the shopper, the contents of the cart, and then imagine the life. She had no experience with romance but liked it above all else. When we saw a couple call one another "honey" or "sweetheart" and exchange a little kiss near the door, she mimicked them. At home she would pause near the refrigerator, give me a soulful look, purse her lips, and call me "sveetheart honeydear" until neither of us could stop laughing.

She was comfortable at the A&P because in Lithuania her parents had a small store where she had sold bread and produce and liquor by the glass to barefoot peasants. I thought of her as a clerk in a Lithuanian 7-Eleven doling out vodka like change. She wanted me to own a store someday—her son, Max, when he died, had already been a partner in a clothing store.

"You'll have more than a store," she told me. "Someday you'll have two stores."

This was a subject of dispute between my grandparents. Rocky didn't want me primed for storekeeping. He had bigger plans. On my outings with him he took me to various teachers, men who he said knew what to teach a boy like me. He would regularly lead me to the apartment of one of these sages, usually a dingy three or four rooms near a gas station. He introduced me in the same way to each of the wise men: "Do something. Teach him. He's growing up like a goy."

I don't know what any of these men might have done. As I think of them now, they were probably bigger disappointments than I was. The itinerant teachers and rabbis who passed through western Michigan in the late 1940s would no doubt have preferred to be elsewhere. How he found so many amazes me. The easiest for me to sidestep were the bearded old men, the *meshulachs*, who appeared at our doorstep before Rosh Hashanah to collect money for widows and yeshivas. They were the traveling salesmen of Jewish charity, their eyes on richer prey than Rocky. I had no problem with them: a quick blessing and that was that. While they talked to me they read bus schedules.

The younger teachers who tutored me for weeks at a time made up a kind of circuit, a pony express of teachers who alighted for a while in the provinces. They would lead a service in Kalamazoo, perform a wedding in Niles, teach a class in Muskegon, all the while doing penance for their mediocrity in the seminary and praying for a better life in a big city. Most of them got their wish, but not before Rocky brought me in and made his plea.

I would sit beside a Hebrew book and a glass of tea, while a wispy man in his thirties would say, "So we'll begin."

We never got beyond beginnings. My heart was too American. While they helped me read and translate Hebrew and Aramaic prayers, I was thinking of baseball. The three or four teachers whom I remember specifically were decent men. They were not very worried about me or my failure; they had their own problems. I remember one young man who was thinking of taking a permanent job; after a few minutes of teaching he quizzed me about rentals in the area. Another was learning to drive. He drew diagrams of a car in traffic and narrated his moves to me. As I stumbled over the Creation and Noah and Abraham's early life, the teachers were as bored as I was. If they had a choice, and the proper training, they would have preferred to be killing chickens.

Rocky didn't take out his anger and disappointment at me, but it became part of the constant feud with Gootie—not that they needed a reason to argue; it was a daily event. There was no suspense in their disagreements: when Rocky and Gootie argued, Rocky always lost.

My father stayed out of all the squabbles, but my mother had inherited Rocky's quick temper and used it against him. She inevitably sided with Gootie. Because the war had separated her parents, when my mother came to America at twelve, someone had to tell her who the dapper fellow in brown-and-white shoes and a gold pocket watch was. She never understood him. In a way, her father remained more a stranger to her than to my sisters and me, who had known him all our lives.

If the argument with Gootie was serious enough, Rocky responded by storming upstairs. The house was a triplex. We lived downstairs, and there were two apartments above. The heat from the coal furnace was erratic on the first floor, almost nonexistent on the second, although with a wall heater, the back apartment was warm enough to rent.

Rocky slept in the front apartment. I don't know when he and Gootie stopped sharing a bed, but my guess was that Max's death had ended that part of their life as well. Sleeping in the empty apartment gave him the privacy he needed to keep his hours, to bed at eight-thirty, up at four.

To get upstairs you had to walk through a long unheated hallway and then up a dark staircase. To go from the warm crowded downstairs filled with the noise of my sisters and their girlfriends and the TV and the bustle of the kitchen to the cold empty upstairs seemed to me a terrible punishment. Usually, after an argument with Gootie, he would retreat to his bedroom but return in an hour or so. When his anger didn't abate, the big job of my childhood was to coax him downstairs, back into the bosom of the family.

Gootie never stayed angry. Sometimes I thought she argued for sport, just to rile him up. When he didn't come down for a meal, she worried. So did I.

I would put on my coat and go upstairs. He was usually sitting at a wooden table covered with a white crocheted cloth, reading the Talmud.

At four and five I was like a little lawyer going to question the prisoner in his cell. On the first trip I would merely listen—let him get out his rage and state the justice of his case. On the second trip, maybe an hour later I would bring food prepared by his enemy wife. He would refuse to touch it.

Then my work began. I had to charm him into eating. He was stubborn and not always hungry. Sometimes I failed.

Depending on the severity of the argument—how injured he felt— he would stay upstairs for hours or even carry on the dispute the following day.

On one occasion it stretched into a second, and then a third, and a fourth day. That battle concerned a housepainter. Rocky had promised the job of painting our house to Ed—one of his Polish co-workers at the bakery. Gootie had struck a deal with Mr. Cooley, a retired man who lived across the street. She had made the deal in Yiddish—I had translated, so I felt partly responsible. Mr. Cooley got the job. I witnessed the handshake.

For Rocky more than honor was at stake. At that time, he clung tenaciously to his part-time job. Ed, his candidate, was one of three people who could squeal to the union. The "bastids" from the union had forced Rocky to retire. He continued to work, secretly. His cousin Phillip, who owned the American Bakery, kept him on part-time. Rocky knew the danger, but he always wanted more hours. Going to the bakery with him was a kind of espionage mission. The union spies we knew might be anywhere. He had only joined the union when he had to, and then, in a matter of months, the union work rules forced him to retire.

Phillip was taking a big chance, Rocky told me. If they caught him, the union could shut down the bakery. I never went in without looking around for the union men, whom Rocky described to me only as "bastids, cokesuckers, and son of a beetches."

While he worked, I would have a doughnut and a glass of milk and all the time keep a lookout. I ate at a little rest area Rocky had set up for me, a stool and some soft flour sacks to lie down on if I wanted to take a nap. I didn't bother him while he worked. I knew better.

There were two other bakers, Joe Post and Ed Wizneski, the one who moonlighted as a painter. Joe weighed over two hundred and tossed seventy-five-pound sacks of flour like marbles, but when he decorated a cake he held the long tube of artificial color delicately, like a paintbrush, and made tiny green and red flowers even when he was looking across the table at Rocky, yelling at him to go faster.

Ed teased Rocky about turning him in to the union. Rocky took it seriously.

"What's your hurry?" Ed would say. "You're not even working, you're not here, you're retired." Rocky tried to ignore the taunts, but he worried that Ed, who also moonlighted as a drunk, would tell the union. He probably considered the housepainting job as a kind of bribe. I tried to explain all of this to Gootie and my mother—it didn't help. They wanted him to retire. Even part-time he was still working thirty hours a week. I understood more than they did how much he loved the bakery.

Usually I had to wait in the salesroom, but when he let me come into the back I could watch the process, sometimes the whole thing, from flour, shortening, water, yeast, and eggs to those crisp shiny breads that emerged.

I watched the rising of the bread like a cartoon. Rocky knew exactly when it was ready for the oven and when to take it out without a clock or a timer.

On cake days he stayed late. Rocky and Joe Post were both cake men. They used a different kind of flour, and on cakes, even Rocky slowed down. They waited until all the breads were done, then readjusted the oven temperature. When they made fresh frosting I always got a taste.

"You gotta know what you're doing when you bake cakes," Rocky said. "Cakes aren't like cookies or doughnuts."

When there was no one else to do it, he made doughnuts, but he hated it. "Doughnuts," he said, "is not baking—it's frying."

I knew them as frycakes. The American Bakery made only one kind, no topping, just fried pieces of dough with a hole in the middle.

Rocky drew the line at cookies. I'd seen him storm away once when Phillip asked him to make ten dozen coconut spots.

"You want cookies," he said, "you don't need a baker. He can make cookies."

He pointed to me. Phillip looked my way. I was excited, I thought he was going to let me do it.

"Don't be so stubborn," Phillip said. "Just ten dozen, how long will it take you?"

Rocky took off his apron and threw it on the table. "C'mon," he said to me. I waited a few seconds in case Phillip decided to ask me, then I ran to catch up.

At home we never made cookies, either. "If you're going to eat all that sugar," he said, "eat something good, a pastry or a cake."

In the front, while I waited for him, I would read a book or have a snack, but when he allowed me in the baking room I watched, riveted by the process before me. I never got tired of it. Staying home couldn't compare with the bakery.

"I'm on your side," I told him. "I want Ed to paint the house."

Downstairs, I lobbied Gootie. She was ready to give in, but my mother hardened her heart: "If you'll stop bringing his food to him, he'll come down when he's hungry," she said. "Just leave him alone."

On the fifth day of the dispute, when he wouldn't even come down to watch "The Original Amateur Hour," my mother gave up. "Tell him that Ed can paint the house," she said. "I can't stand it anymore, he's wearing me out."

I ran upstairs without a jacket to tell him the good news, but he wouldn't budge. His anger had separated itself from the cause, it had taken on an independent life. I couldn't reason with him.

It was only about eight o'clock, but he had already hung his trousers and jacket over the chair at the foot of the bed. Propped on the huge pillow that kept him almost a third of the way to sitting while he slept, he told me he was never coming downstairs again. I believed him.

I went downstairs and returned with my pajamas, two Archie comic books, and my pillow. Later my sister helped me carry up one of the feather beds that Gootie had carted from Russia. He told me to go downstairs, but I refused.

The bedroom had been a kitchen and still was. A porcelain sink separated twin mahogany beds. I settled in across the sink from him. Even though the room had some heat, I could still see my breath. In a few minutes Rocky snored. I was about seven years old, almost asleep myself, when I heard from behind the kitchen wall—the tenants.

I saw them every day as they crossed the yard to the back entrance that led to their apartment. They were newlyweds. She was a small brunette about twenty. I don't remember her name, but his is embedded forever. I heard her moan "Roger" over and over. I wasn't sure what they were doing, but I understood that it mattered.

In the morning Rocky ordered me downstairs. "It's too cold for you up here," he said.

"I like it," I told him, and the next night I was back.

When he saw that I meant business and wouldn't budge, Rocky relented. He let me carry messages back and forth. For two days the bargaining continued. Then we reached a settlement. Ed would scrape the house, Cooley would paint. As chief negotiator, I named my price and I got it. I stayed upstairs. Rocky had a roommate.

Chapter 3

While I lingered in the old world, my sisters went headlong into the melting pot. Years before debate, they figured out democracy by joining clubs. Maxine rose to captain of the Turner School Safety Patrol. Bailey became a junior high student council officer. Encouraged by their examples and my second-grade teacher, who thought that I didn't play enough, my parents urged me to take a big step into America. Reluctantly, I became a Cub Scout.

Mrs. Clark came to our class to recruit for a new den. I knew her. She was the cashier at the Red and White, a small grocery store on Front Street, four blocks from our house. It was the only store that stocked the big brown chunks of root that Rocky ground up for horseradish.

Mrs. Clark was a very heavy woman with blond hair and red lipstick. Her son John was in my class. On the playground he was always the captain of one of the teams, and I was happy to be on his side whenever he chose me.

John had been a Cub Scout the year before in another den and liked it so much that Mrs. Clark wanted to offer all of us the same opportunity.

She asked John to stand in front of the class. He wore the full blue uniform.

"But here"—Mrs. Clark pointed at his right shoulder—"here you can see that there's nothing written in for his den number. Next week we'll have a number that John will wear—so will all of you. Cub Scouts," she said, "is not like school, but it's not like recess, either. It's organized. You'll have fun, and you'll learn things without even realizing that you're learning."

I joined, but there was only one problem. Our den would meet at the Church of St. Peter and St. Paul. Rocky forbade me to go.

"A Jew," he said, "doesn't go to a church."

I argued. "It's not a church, it's a meeting room in a church."

"That's the same thing."

"It is not," I said. "It's just a room with chairs and tables like a school. And there's no priests or nuns, just Mrs. Clark, the den mother."

"First they tell you den mother, pretty soon they'll start talking about a Holy Mother. I know, it was like that in Lithuania."

"They didn't have Cub Scouts in Lithuania," I argued.

"You're right, we didn't waste our time on such things. We studied."

He refused to give his permission, but with my parents and sisters and even Gootie encouraging me, I stood my ground.

"You want to go to a church," Rocky said, "you'll go without me."

I did. My father drove me to the meeting in his truck. I didn't even tell Rocky I was going. I walked up the steps and into the yellow brick building as wary as if I were entering a prison.

I remember that it didn't smell right to me. I walked past stained-glass windows and didn't look up. I headed for the room number that I had written down. I knew it was in the basement, so I just looked for stairs. When I saw them I ran, and when I found the room I opened the door and saw only Mrs. Clark and a few boys in uniform and not a room full of nuns and priests as I half expected. I relaxed. There were chairs and a blackboard and on the table a kite-making display; everything looked like school.

"Hi," Mrs. Clark said, "I'm glad you could make it." She knew, I think, because I had bought only a cap and a compass instead of a full uniform that I was on shaky ground. "You like kites?" she asked. "I hope so. We're having an interesting demonstration."

"Outside?" I asked, hoping it would be so I could tell Rocky that the whole thing took place outdoors and not even mention that I had entered and gone downstairs.

"No!" Mrs. Clark said. "Right there at the table, but next week, after everyone makes one of his own, we'll go outside together and fly them. You'll really like that, everyone does."

She waited until all fourteen boys arrived, then we pledged allegiance to the flag, holding our caps against our hearts, and recited a Cub Scout pledge. Mrs. Clark read a letter from the district director, welcoming us as a new pack. She wrote our number on the blackboard so we could write it down and buy shoulder patches.

"You're in for a special treat tonight," she said. "I told you when I made the announcement at school that we'd be doing kites, but I didn't tell you that we'd be learning from a master kite maker who has been making his own designs for more than twenty years. Let's give him a big Cub Scout welcome."

We did. I clapped as hard as anyone until the side door opened and a bald priest walked in.

"This is Father Dembrowski," Mrs. Clark said. "I know some of you boys go to church here and know him very well. We appreciate your coming in to spend some time with us, Father."

"It's my pleasure, Mrs. Clark," the father said. "I like Cub Scout groups, and I want you to know that all the church grounds and facilities are open to you. But when you start flying your own kites, please stay off the parking lot on Sunday morning or I'll probably lose my job."

I recognized him from the bakery. He was a heavyset bald man about fifty. This was the first time I'd heard him speak English. In the bakery it was always Polish. Rocky had talked to him lots of times. He was one of three or four priests who gave the American Bakery a lot of business. I looked down in case he might recognize me. It felt strange to hear him speaking English.

"Kite making," the father said, "is a challenging and wonderful activity. As Mrs. Clark said, I've been doing it for many years. A well-built kite can give you hours and hours of pleasure, so let's get started."

He walked to his worktable, where there were sticks and paper and string.

While he demonstrated kite making I kept my eye on Mrs. Clark to see if she would put on a nun's habit. When she noticed me staring she motioned with her hand for me to watch the father.

I did. He had fast, nimble fingers. We all watched as he tied the plywood and then stapled thin paper to the wood. It took him only a few minutes.

"When you make them at home," he said, "don't worry about the stapling—I can do that for you here. Just pick whatever design you want and cut it to size."

He held up a simple brown kite. "There's about a nickel's worth of material here," the father said, "and if you're careful, you can fly it all year. Can't beat that, can you?"

Each of us got a little kit, plywood, string, and paper. A gift from Father Dembrowski. I snuck mine into the house and put it into the drawer where my shirts and Rocky's long underwear lay side by side. It was the only drawer long enough to hold the sticks. I hid the packet at the bottom of the drawer and took it out only when I was sure I would be alone.

I wanted to make a good kite and was sure that I could. The priest's instructions were clear. But every time I put the two pieces of plywood on the floor and started to tie one against the other, I didn't see a kite, I saw a cross. The more solidly I tied the sticks, the more guilty I felt. I angled first one stick a little, then another. The shape I finally tied into place was much closer to an X than a cross.

Rocky didn't mention the Cub Scouts. I think he assumed I had never gone. The next week I snuck the kite out and walked to the church. Mrs. Clark had my hat and compass waiting for me.

"You can order the rest of the uniform whenever you want," she said, "there's no hurry. This is enough to make you official." She put the hat on me. I remained a proud Cub Scout for about fifteen minutes.

When I brought my frame to Father Dembrowski for stapling, he shook his head. "You'll have to redo this," he said. "It will never fly. Don't you remember what I showed you last week?"

His fingers went at my knot, and before my eyes my kite became a crucifix. I ran for the door.

"What's the matter?" Mrs. Clark called out. "Don't you feel good?"

I was up the stairs and out of the church before she could move her big body from the chair.

At home, I found Rocky cleaning the birdbath. I confessed.

"I went to church," I said, "but I didn't make a cross."

He put down the hose and stopped scrubbing the ceramic bowl. I told him about Father Dembrowski and the kite.

"You became one of them?" he asked. I had forgotten that I was wearing my blue beanie.

"Just a Cub Scout," I said, "not a goy."

"And you want to do this?"

I nodded. "Everyone in my class is in the den."

"C'mon," he said.

We walked to the Church of St. Peter and St. Paul. I wouldn't go in. Rocky did.

"I thought we weren't supposed to go in," I reminded him.

"We're not," he said, "but if you're wearing a hat, it's not so bad."

I sat on the steps and waited for him. Mrs. Clark came out first. She put a big arm around me. "I'm so sorry, honey. I didn't know. Your grandpa and Father D talked it all out in Polish. Father D didn't mean anything about religion—he was just talking about kites."

She waited on the steps with me until Rocky and Father D came out. They were still talking Polish. Behind them marched my den, everyone carrying a kite. John Clark handed me mine, bent back to the X I had originally made.

We flew the kites on the church parking lot. My misshapen one got into the air, but as I ran to give it space it sank and stuck on the antenna of a 1947 Plymouth, the priest's car.

After that we met at Mrs. Clark's house. She and John lived in three rooms above the Red and White.

We met at the store and watched while she locked the door; then we followed her up the steep staircase to her three-room apartment for our snack. She carried two wet glass bottles of milk. Her body took up the entire width of the staircase. She passed the banisters the way semi trucks pass each other on a narrow highway.

We were seven years old, a time when everything is funny, especially fat people. But I don't remember anyone ever laughing about Mrs. Clark. She had great dignity and character. So did John. I didn't know what to call it then, but I knew John was someone you could always trust.

She passed out milk and cookies, then John collected the cups and washed them. They didn't even have a television set. The only decoration in the room that barely held all of us was Mr. Clark's picture on the wall. We saw him in his uniform, and we knew he'd died in Europe defending his country. We were little boys in blue beanies drinking milk in the apartment of a hero. It made me feel as if I were serving my country, too. A few weeks later I bought the trousers and shirt and an official whistle. That year I made a straw broom and a lamp, and I learned to climb a rope hand over hand. But I never forgot the kite. The next year, when it was time for Boy Scouts, I stayed home.

Chapter 4

When I was twelve Rocky gave up on my intellect. My approaching Bar Mitzvah made him face reality. I would become a man, but not a rabbi.

Tenderly, he gave me the news that was not news to me. "Not everyone can do it," he said. "In Europe you would have had a chance."

"In Europe," I reminded him, "I would have been dead."

He had an alternate plan. He believed in apprenticeships. "You can be a professional man," he said. "You'll never have to work nights."

He walked with me to the Rexall drugstore a block from our house. I waited at the soda fountain while Rocky talked to the pharmacist, a man I knew only as Doc. Doc had two gold teeth like fangs when he opened his mouth wide, warning us not to read the comic books.

A tall man on level ground, Doc was a giant when he stood in the elevated pharmacist's booth and looked out at his goods, his eyes more observant than today's electronic cameras.

He stepped down from his perch—he and Rocky walked toward me.

I sat on a round stool, staring straight at a tube of Unguentine, trying to look as professional as I could.

"Your grandpa tells me," Doc said, "that you want to be a druggist."

Rocky had coached me in advance. I had a line. "If he asks you something," Rocky had said, "just say, 'I'm ready to work.' That's all."

I nodded.

"Can I trust you around the comic books?"

"I'm ready to work," I said.

"A lot of sick people come in here, you know that," Doc said. "You'll be exposed."

"I'm ready to work."

"You may be ready," he said, "but you're too young. It's against the law."

"Sonofabeetches," Rocky said. "The unions are ruining him, too. Give the boy a chance, Doc. I want him to be something."

"I told you, Rocky, I can't hire him, but . . . maybe . . ." He stared at me.

"I'm ready to work," I said.

"You can hang around," Doc said. "You can learn the ropes."

He walked behind the soda fountain to the stainless-steel surface where the soda flavorings and the milk shake machines were. He handed me a damp red rag.

I held it in two hands as if it were a money belt.

While I wiped the sticky surface of the soda fountain, Doc went back to his druggist's perch and Rocky, accepting my failure and my limitations, walked to the American Bakery satisfied that he had done what had to be done. I would be a professional man.

At the Rexall store I also swept the floor, straightened the shelves, and stayed alert for learning the secrets of the druggist's trade.

"If you're a good worker," Rocky had told me, "he'll take you in the back and show you how he makes the medicines. Once you know that, you'll understand science."

I waited, but science eluded me. Doc didn't fill that many prescriptions. Most of the time he worked crossword puzzles from some of the magazines on the rack. After tearing out the puzzle pages he'd put the magazine back for sale.

"Nobody'll miss it," he said. Though I was careful not to risk my job by reading the comic books, Doc didn't seem to mind if I read the newspaper or the magazines. Since I was about to become a scientist myself, I began to notice how often Albert Einstein appeared in the news. I read everything I could about him in *Life* and *Look* and *Colliers* and the *Grand Rapids Press* and reading about the great physicist whetted my appetite to understand prescriptions.

One day I finally asked Doc when he was going to show me the compounds.

"Okay," he said. "You wanna know medicine—I'm gonna show you."

He told Jerry, the fountain worker, to watch the entire store. He led me, not just behind the counter, but into the back room, where there were boxes full of cigarettes and candy and toothpaste and Vaseline alongside the glass bottles of medicine.

"There's two big things wrong with the world," Doc said. "One is war, the other is the clap."

He opened a bottle and put a blue-and-orange capsule into my hand. "Look at that," he said. "Know what you're holding?"

I didn't know. "Penicillin," Doc said.

He took the capsule out of my hand and dropped it back in the bottle. "I've seen you reading about Einstein in *Life*."

I nodded.

"It's all baloney. I mean, he might have invented the atomic bomb all right, but it wasn't the bomb that saved us—it was penicillin.

"The Germans had a plot to give everybody the clap. You're too young—I'm not gonna tell you how, but once they knew we had penicillin they called it off. So what do you think is more important, the bomb or penicillin?"

"Penicillin," I said.

"Don't forget it," Doc said.

I tried not to, but all the magazines had pictures of the flash of light and the mushroom cloud. Doc's blue-and-orange capsules couldn't compete with all that power.

When I read that Einstein didn't believe in God and never went to synagogue, it strengthened my own resolve. I became absolutely certain, in spite of Doc, that I liked Einstein even more than penicillin. The great scientist gave me confidence. One Saturday when Rocky was hurrying me to get ready for synagogue, I dropped my own atom bomb. I refused to go.

He left without me, and that afternoon we had it out. With Einstein in my corner I denounced religion.

Rocky called me an *apikoros*, the Hebrew version of the Greek *epicurean*, and he stopped talking to me. He didn't wake me, he didn't take me to the bakery with him, he didn't bring pastries home. When I came into the living room to watch baseball or wrestling with him, he left.

The rest of the family wisely stayed out of it. It complicated matters that at this time I was actively preparing for my Bar Mitzvah. Whatever I believed, I certainly intended to go through with that. I wanted the presents.

"Call off the Bar Mitzvah," he said. "An *apikoros* doesn't need a Bar Mitzvah."

I refused, and my family backed me up.

"Go ahead," Rocky said, "have a Bar Mitzvah, but I won't be there."

We went down to the wire. My parents, the rabbi, nobody could convince either of us to give in. I said it was science versus faith, a phrase I read in *Life* magazine. More likely I was getting even for all the years of stale tutoring. Ten days before I became a man, the drugstore got its first shipment of 3-D comic books. There had been rumors that they were coming for months, and other than the Bar Mitzvah nothing excited me more. Sharkey, who distributed magazines and tobacco, whetted my appetite. He had seen one. "Superman looks like he's flying off the page to punish you," he said. "You've never seen anything like it."

There were already 3-D movies. I had seen ads for *Bwana Devil*, but it was downtown at the Majestic and too expensive. I had to wait until it came to the Town on Bridge Street as part of a triple feature.

In the weeks of my apprenticeship at the Rexall store, I had never, while on duty, opened a comic book. The day the 3-Ds arrived, I couldn't resist. I bought one for a dollar, ten times the price of a regular comic. There were five 3-D titles, but Mighty Mouse did me in. I wanted to see the red line that signified his speed in three dimensions.

When Doc caught me, I had opened the cellophane packet that

contained the red-and-blue three-dimensional glasses and I was sitting on a pile of *Police Gazette* issues, holding the comic at an angle to feel the full force of Mighty Mouse coming off the page.

Doc yanked the comic out of my hands. I held on so tightly that one of the pages ripped in half. He pulled the glasses off my face.

"Get out," he said. "You know the rules."

I ran home and went to my bedroom before I started to cry. When Rocky came in I was really sobbing. He still wasn't talking to me. He left the room, but in a minute he came back. He sat down beside me.

"What happened?" he asked.

"Doc kicked me out," I said. "I'll never be a druggist." I told him why.

Later, Jerry, who worked at the fountain, told me what happened. Rocky walked to the back, into the employees only area, where Doc was mixing a prescription.

"He went at Doc with his fists," Jerry said. "It was the funniest thing I ever saw. The old guy wanted to fight. Doc didn't want to hit him, so he just kept running around the Hallmark card display and finally he yelled for me to watch the store and he ran out the door."

I was still crying when Rocky came home.

"It was his fault," Rocky said. "The druggist put Einstein into your head. I'm glad you won't be a druggist."

He rubbed my back until I stopped crying.

At my Bar Mitzvah he sat in the first row and motioned for me to sing louder. He corrected my four mistakes in the Hebrew reading. I gave my speech in Yiddish, a language that only my family and a few of the old people understood. I spoke about what was on my mind, the atomic bomb. I compared it to the Flood in Noah's time and reminded my audience that nobody promised rainbows after bombs.

After the Bar Mitzvah, I didn't flaunt Einstein and Rocky was equally discreet about God. For prescriptions we went to the Cut-Rate store on Leonard Street.

Chapter 5

*T*he way Rocky had blazed our trail in America, my sisters led the way in education. First Bailey, seven years older, then Maxine, two and a half years ahead of me, won scholarships to the University of Michigan. My parents expected me to follow in the footsteps of the girls.

Their success gave me greater responsibility. When I was a high school senior Bailey was already working in Detroit—Maxine had a boyfriend and would clearly be moving far from home when she graduated. I felt the burden of my grandparents' loneliness. If I went away to college, my parents would miss me, but they had other things to do in the world. Rocky and Gootie didn't. The thought of leaving them made me ambivalent about college.

Instead of meeting that subject head-on, we discussed food. At that time there was no kosher food regularly available at the university. At home our meat came every month from Detroit, and Rocky baked the bread—our packaged goods carried the little circled *u* that identified it as rabbinically approved. We never ate out.

"You'll get TB," Gootie warned me. "You won't eat and you'll cough up blood, God forbid."

"TB comes from germs," I told her, "and now it's curable."

"You believe everything they tell you. TB is still TB, only here they call it cancer."

My sisters began to eat nonkosher at college. "You can, too," my mother said. "You have to."

My break with God had been easy—merely a spiritual matter. Forbidden food was another story. When it came to eating I remained observant enough to be a rabbi.

As unhappy as Gootie was with the idea of my leaving, her greater fear was that I would starve. For this dilemma she called in the family expert, her brother Joe. Sixty years before I graduated from Union High, Joe had served in the quartermaster corps of the imperial Russian army. That experience now came in handy.

"Tell him what you did," Gootie requested of her brother, a retired farmer who now lived in Muskegon, forty miles to the west. He was about seventy-five and looked like Santa without the beard. The combination of short legs and a substantial belly made it hard for Joe to reach the accelerator of his Ford and still see over the wheel. Usually we drove to Muskegon to visit him, but for this emergency he squeezed behind the steering column and came to us.

He arrived on a Sunday in late April after I had been officially admitted to the University of Michigan. The admission and the scholarship put flesh on Gootie's theoretical worries. In five months I would be gone. She needed a plan.

She assembled us in the backyard on the aluminum lawn chairs that we'd bought with S&H green stamps. She sat me across from her brother so I would get the full effect of his advice. There was a lawn chair for Rocky, too, but he didn't join us. He knew the subject, and he would have no part of it. Gootie had been trying unsuccessfully to gain his approval on the grounds of health.

Though I was in good shape, you couldn't tell by looking. At seventeen I had already reached my full height, five feet four inches, but my weight lagged. On a good day I could top one hundred pounds; still, in my own eyes I was strong and quite an athlete.

"Four years without eating meat," Gootie said. "It will be like a concentration camp."

Joe sipped his hot tea. He kept the sugar cube in his mouth, a habit left over from his army days.

Gootie introduced the subject. "In Russia," she said, "it was the army that stole the boys. Here it's worse—the colleges take away the girls, too, but the problem is the same. What can a Jew eat?"

Joe heard his cue. "I ate everything," he said, "except the pork. If I hadn't . . ." He looked heavenward.

"He would have been dead," Gootie added. She wanted to make sure I didn't miss the point. "Tell him what to do," she said.

Joe put down his teacup to reenact dinner in the Russian army.

Rocky had come outside. He stood near the driveway a few feet away and listened.

"First of all," Joe said, "they don't give you meat every day. When they do, it comes on a stick like a Popsicle. You can't say 'I want this one' or that one; the cook hands you a stick and that's that. You eat what you get and you're glad to have it. When you get pork on a stick you go up to someone else who's got beef and you ask him to trade."

"What did you do if nobody would trade?" I asked.

"That never happened," Joe said. "All goyim love pork."

"How could you be sure you were trading for beef?"

"I smelled it first," Joe said, "but you can never really know. If you're hungry enough, it doesn't make any difference."

In his eyes I could see the rueful expression, the nostalgia for his own days at seventeen, suddenly alive.

"Eat everything," he said. "It won't hurt you."

Rocky, moving quickly from the driveway, picked up Joe's aluminum chair by its webbed seat and attacked. I got a hand on the frame, but the webbing hit Joe on the side of the head. His teacup bounced on the grass. Gootie screamed. It took all my strength to hold Rocky while Joe ran to his Ford.

"You doity son of a beetch!" Rocky yelled. "You'd still eat *chazzir*."

When he reached his four-door Ford, Joe took a deep breath and slipped behind the wheel like a teenager.

———•———

In the summer before my freshman year, I went to Ann Arbor for three days of orientation. I took the Greyhound bus. I promised Gootie that I would eat everything.

I stayed in a dormitory room and thought I smelled pork everywhere. I took tests in math and Spanish and English, but my anxiety was about the dining room, not the classroom.

I roomed on the third floor with a group of other Michigan boys. They were accustomed to cafeterias. For my first dinner I squeezed into a crowded elevator and then followed everyone to the dining hall. I tried to decide which of the hulking eighteen-year-olds around me I'd trade my pork to.

I walked through the line, imitating those ahead of me. I picked a salad, avoided the Jell-O, which I knew contained boiled animal hooves. When it came to the main course I froze. A woman in a hairnet finally pushed a plate at me—potatoes with a little pool of gravy in the middle and meat.

I went to a table by myself, but in seconds the other seats filled up. The boys' dormitory was jammed with freshmen-to-be, and I was determined to be one of them. I chewed the tiny green salad with gusto. Then I lifted my fork to the gray-brown gravy and mixed it throughout the potatoes. I listened to the conversation around me, hoping someone would name the main course, but they were talking about Plato.

When the other eaters were almost finished I finally had the courage to ask.

"Meatloaf," one said.

"Hamloaf," said another. They bussed their trays.

"Whatever it is," the meatloaf man said, "it sucks."

I waited until my tablemates left the room, then I carried my tray to the garbage. I hadn't even touched a drop of gravy.

In my three days of orientation I ate only breakfast cereals. I came home pale and hungry.

"That's it," Gootie said. "He can't go to college."

I'd never seen her happier. I was ready to agree. I was so worried about what I could eat that I did badly on all my exams. The counselor assigned to me told me he didn't know how I'd gotten a scholarship. He advised me to go to Grand Rapids Junior College and take remedial English.

"You're going to Ann Arbor," my mother said, "and you'll eat like everyone else, and you'll be smart. What do tests know?"

Gootie plugged for junior college. "You can go there," she said, "and come home for lunch."

"It's only a two-year college," I reminded her.

"You can learn plenty in two years," she said.

I was leaning toward staying home, but as I struggled to decide my father reminded me of what happened when he took me to my first big league game.

I was ten, and we went to see the Tigers play the Red Sox. We left home at six A.M. so we'd be in Detroit early enough to watch all of batting practice.

It was a five-hour drive to Detroit. I was too excited to sleep the night before. For breakfast I had only thin cocoa. I carried my glove, hoping for a foul ball and my Scripto pencil for autographs just in case I ran into Al Kalina or Ted Williams in the parking lot. At a rest stop in central Michigan I left my lunch on a picnic bench. I wanted to go to my first big league game without the burden of a half-pound tuna sandwich on yellow challah. I wanted my hands free for pop fouls, in my lap I wanted only a scorecard.

By the time we got to the ball park it was the fast of Yom Kippur on the backseat. My father circled Briggs Stadium, looking for a parking place. "There it is," he said. Weak and dizzy, I looked up to see the dark green stadium surrounded by a rotting ghetto. A row of solemn black men held placards stating *Parking $1.00* and pointed to their backyards.

My stomach ached. My fingers were hardly strong enough to unlock the door. "You've got to eat something," my father said. He turned away from the stadium toward a bleak business district.

We couldn't go too far or we'd miss out on the parking and the batting practice. My father stopped at a kosher-style deli.

I was so hungry that I left my baseball glove in the car. The waiter told me that the hot dogs were kosher, but I also noticed every variety of swine on his menu.

I ordered a Coke. My father, almost in tears, begged me to eat so I could enjoy the game.

"Tell him to eat, please," he asked the waiter.

The waiter gave me a "Let the little bastard starve" look and returned to the kitchen.

Then a middle-aged waitress came through the swinging varnished doors. "Honey," she said, "come with me."

She pulled my head off the counter and took me into the kitchen. She let me watch while she put two kosher hot dogs into a thick plastic bag and then boiled them in that bag.

She produced a packaged rye bread and pointed out the vegetable shortening. She brought out a side dish of vegetarian baked beans and sat next to me while I ate. She even gave me some hard candy for dessert.

"Those hot dogs were kosher," my father said of that incident, "but you almost spoiled it for yourself by being so stubborn. That was just a doubleheader. This time it's your education. You'll have plenty of chances to keep kosher, you can do it for the rest of your life, but if you don't go to college now, you'll never go."

He walked me outside to his Dodge truck, which he kept in a cement block garage across the street from our house. He unlocked the cab and opened the glove compartment. He took out the pair of tiny yellow mittens that I had prized when I was about five.

"My work gloves," I said.

"Every time I get a new truck, I toss 'em into the glove compartment. They remind me," he said, "that I don't want you to be a truck driver."

In September my parents drove me to Ann Arbor. They helped me unload my belongings in South Quad, and then, for the first time in my life, they took me out to dinner.

My mother had done some research. She asked my sisters and the parents of children who she knew had gone to Michigan. She wanted the name of the best restaurant in town.

I wondered why my father wore his light blue suit and a tie and my mother her best flowered dress. I thought it was to impress the other parents. They didn't tell me until I was in the car that our destination was the Sugar Bowl.

By the time we got there about eight, the restaurant, on Main Street in downtown Ann Arbor, was empty. I later learned it usually was. The Sugar Bowl was a huge high-ceilinged place with plaster columns and walls of two-tone green. A Greek family owned it, and they all worked there. The menu came in a padded red cover. It felt like a textbook.

"Everyone says this is the best," my mother said, as Demetra, our waitress, ushered us to an eight-person booth. All the booths were that size or larger. My feet barely touched the ground. I felt as if I were on an island.

I had, of course, been in restaurants—the coffee shop variety—but I'd never had to face a menu. I had ordered only orange juice or ice cream or a Coke. Now the pressure was on.

My parents tried to pretend it was an everyday event, just an American mom and dad taking their college boy out to dinner. My mother was cheerful; she chatted about her cousin Mamie, who told her about the Sugar Bowl. Mamie had been there during the Depression.

Demetra's English was not great. "Welcome, scholars," she said. We had to repeat every order, and I think she wrote them on the pad in Greek.

"He'll have a steak," my mother said, "the best one you've got."

They worked at being casual. My father talked about the Michigan football team, about the beautiful dormitory my sister Bailey had lived in. He reminded me to give him a copy of the combination to my bike lock. We killed time while in the dark kitchen of the Sugar Bowl, my steak sizzled.

The only full restaurant meals I could recall were at the synagogue. Every year, as a fund-raising event, a speaker came from New York. Women from the sisterhood cooked. We ate on rented tables in the social hall and sat on folding chairs donated by the Alt Mortuary.

It was expensive, maybe twenty or thirty dollars a plate, but my mother wanted me to go to these events. I went during the heyday of my sisters' debating career. Although I didn't take debate, my mother still had hopes that the example of those pitchmen and moralists whom the synagogue paid two hundred dollars and up would someday inspire me to great oratory.

Demetra arrived with my dinner beneath a steel cover. She laid the meat in front of me, surrounded by steaming mashed potatoes and green beans boiled to a pallor. I had heard of T-bones, and now I saw one. I recognized the *T* surrounded by fat and gristle, caught a glimpse of the dark marrow.

"It looks delicious," my mother said as she sipped her orange juice.

My father raised his coffee cup. "*L'chaim*," he said.

Their bravery put a lump in my throat. My father's grandmother left Pennsylvania in the 1880s to return to Poland because she didn't trust the kosher food in America. Gootie's stepgrandmother lived in Brooklyn beyond the age of one hundred without ever tasting canned food.

Our family history was studded with such culinary denial. In our house, fast days were big events—not only Yom Kippur. Rocky fasted for the destruction of the Temple and in sympathy with Queen Esther. Gootie, a libertine like me, checked cabbage and broccoli for weevils. She sifted through dry lentils individually, and she put marks with a file on the silverware so she could tell meat from milk cutlery even in the dark.

I caught my mother staring at the steak. That T-bone was not meat, it was a border. She and my father and all my ancestors sat on one side of the table—the steak and I on the other. Demetra, who had been in Ann Arbor for only three months, sat in a booth across from us, missing Greece and waiting to see if we'd want dessert.

It was already eight-twenty. My father had a four-hour drive home and then on Monday a grueling 250-mile round trip in the truck to buy scrap from his best customer, the Kysor Heater Company.

"Don't let it get cold," my mother said. I thought she might reach across the table and cut the steak into chunks for me as if I were a three-year-old, but she didn't. She looked away from me at the plaster of paris frieze on the wall where Greek heroes with lidded eyes reminded other diners of classical dignity.

I cut, I bit, I chewed. My mother held her breath. I swallowed. I thought they would both applaud. After the first bite I ate everything on one side of the long bone. It was a love feast. I did it for them, they did it for me.

They drove home satisfied that I would not starve in college. In the dormitory I unpacked my clothes and didn't vomit.

My roommate, a muscular sophomore from Detroit, had lived in the dormitory the year before. He had friends and spent the evening in one of the lounges playing bridge. About midnight he returned.

"What did you do?" he asked.

"My parents took me out for a steak dinner."

"Lucky you," he said.

Chapter 6

As an undergraduate I had, for the first time, roommates my own age, and I did not starve. I began graduate school at Stanford in September 1964. In October my father suffered what he said was a mild heart attack. He hired a driver to help him, but he expected to be at full strength in a few months.

When I came home for winter vacation in December he looked well. My first night home, we watched a Michigan basketball game together. The Wolverines had a great team that year led by Cazzie Russel and Bill Buntin.

That September my father had driven to California with me and we'd spent one night in Las Vegas. He'd won two hundred dollars shooting craps and another hundred at blackjack. He was wonderfully relaxed and knew his way around the crap shooting table. While my hot hands had protected the chips, he'd enjoyed the game and the glamorous Las Vegas setting. We'd talked about going again the following fall. He didn't understand exactly what I was doing at Stanford, where I had entered the Ph.D. program in English.

"What does a doctor of philosophy do?" he'd asked. We knew dentists and chiropodists, and M.D.s, but no doctors of philosophy.

"They teach in colleges," I'd said. I was a little tentative because I wasn't sure if they did anything else. I intended to be a writer, but I didn't know how to become one. I thought that getting a Ph.D. would, at least, keep me close to books.

I was upstairs shaving when I heard my mother scream. I ran to their room. My father struggled for breath. His back arched, his fists were clenched. My mother called an ambulance. He couldn't talk. I put my mouth over his and tried to breathe into him. There was blue shaving gel on my face, and some of it smeared onto his suddenly pale cheek. I didn't just breathe into him, I blew with all my might. From the back of his throat I heard a sound that was like a handful of those Las Vegas chips clinking against one another. It was the death rattle. I blew it away.

In a few seconds his lips moved. In a minute he tried to sit up. By the time the ambulance arrived he didn't even want to go to the hospital, but he did go and he stayed, and in the next seven weeks there were two more such episodes as his blood-starved heart shuddered.

I didn't return to Stanford. I stayed to do his work and to visit him in the hospital. Although I had almost tasted his death, it hadn't convinced me. I was twenty-three, and death, to me, still meant Max's tombstone. I knew my father would recover and live for a long time. He looked fine, and he didn't want me to stay away from school.

"The scrap business isn't for you," he said. "Go back to California, I'll be okay in a little while."

He wasn't okay in January or in February. He remained in the hospital, and on the last day of the month, just after midnight, his heart stopped. He was fifty-nine.

Rocky, who fought with everyone else, never had a run-in with my father. He lost another son.

Gootie survived my father by just over a year. During that year I took over the truck, becoming little Sam, shoveling up steel and aluminum shavings in machine shops in Big Rapids and Lakeview or standing beside the loading dock at the Kysor factory in Cadillac while union men driving high-lows loaded our dump truck with barrels of oily brass shavings and the carcasses of used radiators.

By then, the girls were married. Maxine lived in California, Bailey in Minnesota. My mother, Rocky, and I remained in an empty house full of memories. My father's months in the hospital and then Gootie's were uninsured. Medicare took effect the week that Gootie died. I had to keep working on the truck. In the glove compartment the yellow mittens were still there, but I didn't need them to remind me that this wasn't what my father had wished.

I hated the small talk with the workers in the machine shops and garages. The various grades of aluminum and brass and bronze all looked, to my eyes, like what they were called—junk. I dreamed of a way out. My year and a half at Stanford seemed, from my seat in the Dodge, like paradise. I couldn't imagine ever again having the leisure to imagine. I dismissed my farfetched notion of becoming a writer; nothing was farther from my mind. Yet the only thing that gave me satisfaction that year were my daydreams, the unwritten stories that kept me company for three hours between Grand Rapids and Cadillac.

About six months after my father's death my mother tried a daring experiment. Our business was teetering. Competitors understood my inexperience and offered higher prices to our customers, especially the Kysor factory in Cadillac. When my father had started buying their scrap, Kysor was a small machine shop; now they were listed on the New York Stock Exchange.

While my father was alive the customers were secure. In a business known for uncertain weights, his honesty was beyond doubt. Some of the factories didn't even weigh what they sold to him, and the men on the shop floor, the foremen and lathe operators and maintenance crews of those small factories, knew him as their friend. He spoke their language, I didn't.

My mother didn't know she was a feminist when one Monday she and the driver secretly arranged to start early. At three A.M. she stepped up into the cab of the truck to sit beside Francis and ride north. By five, when my alarm went off and I read her note in the kitchen, she was well past Big Rapids and busy studying a list of metals and prices. That day, a fifty-seven-year-old, four-foot-eleven-inch grandmother oversaw eleven tons of mixed metals and steel scrap.

She went out of her way to personally greet every one of my father's friends in the factory. She told the purchasing agent that she knew others were trying to take our business and asked him to give us time to learn what we had to do. She wore slacks and a wool sweater. Her hair was as white as Rocky's, and she had his energy. On the loading dock the men had to keep her from trying to move the barrels by hand.

When she came back with the load of metal, she drove a hard bargain at the junkyard. She asked the manager of the yard to write out the price of every metal, then she took out the list the purchasing agent at Kysor had given her—the prices our competitors were offering for yellow brass and number two copper and aluminum clippings.

When she came home fourteen hours after she had set out, there were smudges on her slacks and grease under her nails. She had new prices, a penny and a half raise on metals, five dollars more a ton on the steel. Her earnings that day were about $300 more than mine would have been.

"Go back to school," she said.

I waited a few weeks to make sure she really could run the scrap business, then I left not for California but back to Ann Arbor, and I took along my old roommate, ninety-three by then.

He was happy to accompany me. At home he had outlived his town and his time. He had been among the founders of the synagogue in Grand Rapids, but to the middle-aged and young members he was merely a weird old man sitting in the last row, chanting prayers that long ago had been removed from the liturgy by the ever more progressive congregation.

Yet at ninety-three he was scarcely different from the way he'd seemed to me all my life. It was as if his body had reached a certain point in aging and then gone on hold. He didn't remain young; he was more like a permanent seventy. His white hair thinned but stayed. He had good color and muscle tone. He didn't wear glasses. He was strong. He wanted to work.

In Ann Arbor I rented better housing than I could afford, a suburban garden apartment, close to a bus stop and a mall and far from the campus, teeming in those years with antiwar protest.

When I met Debby, Rocky had already been in Ann Arbor with me for a year. He made friends at the synagogue and in the apartment building. He sometimes walked the three miles to campus. He baked for a few neighbors, and they told others in the complex. On some days he kept busy baking in three or four apartments. When she could get away, my mother came to spend weekends with us. I felt lucky to have been able to return to a version of the life I wanted without abandoning him. I didn't want to change the way things were.

By the time I walked back into my apartment on that late summer night in 1968, he was already asleep. I heard his snoring, which began as a whistle and ended as a soft puff of breath. I had been hearing that sound all my life. Behind the door there was one item that Debby had left behind, a silky robe. It had a blue background and multicolored stripes like Joseph's coat in Genesis. I put it on a hanger and tiptoed into the closet. I hung it on my side.

In the morning he did not mention the girl. I'm sure he considered the matter finished—out of sight, out of mind. He concentrated on what was in front of him. When I got out of bed at seven he had already baked a dozen rolls, cleaned the kitchen, and taken out the garbage. I knew he was angry because he was reading the Help Wanted section of the *Ann Arbor News*. He folded the paper into quarters and stared at the ads. He wore no glasses and handled the small print without difficulty. He wet the tip of the pencil with his mouth and circled an ad here and there.

Whenever he was mad at me he looked for a job immediately, and whenever I was mad at him I delivered a lecture. These were our styles— and neither one worked. Nobody would hire him, and he wouldn't listen to me, but that didn't stop us.

There were no good mornings. The minute I stepped into the kitchen he headed for the bedroom—not to avoid me, but to make the bed. He loved order, not cleanliness. He washed the dishes badly—bits of flour and dough clung to the pots. He didn't fluff the pillows or straighten the sheets, but he got the bedspread on and tucked it in. I often thought, when I was a teenager and wanted on vacation mornings to luxuriate in my bed, that he wouldn't have minded my sleeping if only he could have made up the bed while I was still in it.

He would stand for no impediments to his sense of the way things should be. And where girls were concerned, until Debby, I had not tested him.

I hardly knew Debby, yet I had brought her back to our apartment. Maybe I had already decided in the crowded ballroom of the peace movement that she was the one, and maybe he suspected as much when, stepping out in the middle of the night, he saw a living room full of her clothes. Of course he hated the disorder; that I knew. But a girl in my life would be the greatest disorder of all. I should have understood that and searched for some way to reassure him. Instead, while my angry busy grampa cleaned the pots and then mopped the kitchen floor, I lectured him on manners and morals, circa 1968. Between bites of cinnamon roll I explained modern romance.

"First, there is nothing wrong with bringing a girl to your apartment. Second, everyone is entitled to privacy. Third, under any circumstances you don't throw a person out."

"You're lucky," he said, "that I woke up or she'd be here right now with a policeman."

"A policeman?"

"Yes," he repeated, "a policeman. You bring a girl to your house and carry her clothes in and then you don't marry her—they'll put you in jail for breach of promise."

"This is not 1910. There's no such thing as breach of promise, girls don't expect you to marry them, and anyway, I don't even know her. I was just giving her a place to store her clothes."

"She needs storage," he said. "They got lockers at the bus station. She won't sue the bus station." He took the mop outside to dry in the sun and left for his morning walk.

"It's not over," I yelled to him as he slammed the door, and I hoped I was telling the truth.

All that summer I was studying for my preliminary exams. I had to know English literature from Chaucer in 1400 to Henry James in 1916. My reading list was nine single-spaced typed pages, and a lot of the books were multivolumes.

Of course it was impossible to know it all, but three or four months of solid reading wouldn't hurt my chances. That was my job for the summer—to lie on the gray vinyl couch, a thick book resting on my belly and a yellow highlighter in my right hand every once in a while darting toward a line of Shakespeare or a paragraph of Ruskin.

Rocky couldn't take it. "Lazy son of a beetch," he called me.

"It's my job. I'm getting paid to do it." It was true. I had a summer study fellowship.

"You lay there doing this . . ." He imitated with his finger my gesture of underlining. "Look, I'm working, too." He mimicked me, underlining the empty air.

What I was doing, in graduate school, reading while I lay on the gray couch, did not, to him, constitute a job. Every day I woke up, ate, showered, and went to the couch. When he came back from his walk he went to the kitchen and grumbled loud enough for me to hear, "Lazy good-for-nothing."

That didn't bother me, but when he put on the TV to watch the news or "Concentration" or "Jeopardy!" I would go to the bedroom, which was not as well lighted or as comfortable. When his shows were over he would make lunch for me, usually herring and onions and coffee. I had been eating that for so long that it didn't seem strange to me, but every now and then, when he packed me a lunch, I noticed people moving away when I spread my feast on the lawn or at a crowded table in the Student Union.

He ate his big meal at noon and then took a nap. I liked to stick around in the mornings to keep him company. Even if my face was buried in a book, I was still there.

It finally got through to me that he was happier if I left. When I ate the oatmeal as fast as I could, almost chugged the hot coffee, loaded my briefcase so that it weighed me down, and hurried away, he believed I was working.

I would stay away until suppertime. We'd watch the Walter Cronkite news together, then he'd cook soft-boiled or scrambled eggs and start to get ready for bed. He was always asleep by eight-thirty and usually up by four. He kept his bakery hours.

Twice a week I helped him take a bath. Tuesdays a quickie, just for hygiene; the main bath came on Friday afternoon. In honor of the approaching Sabbath, Rocky soaked. Tub lifeguard was a new job for me. At home, in the big claw-footed bath, he had been confident. The apartment tub, though half the size, required him to enter at a steep angle, and there were no sides to grab.

On Fridays he waited for me, even when I had late classes that sometimes kept me on campus until four or five. I only had to help him enter and leave, but once I saw his hair-washing technique, I became an active participant. His method was quick. He ran the bar of soap over his hair as if it were an arm or a leg. To rinse, instead of using the faucet, he leaned back as far as he could.

I introduced shampoo, and when I brought in the teakettle to pour warm water over his head for the rinse, he closed his eyes and held his breath.

Neither of us was self-conscious about nakedness. Our lives were so close that helping him bathe didn't seem much more intimate than listening to him snore or pray. When he was up to his armpits in hot water, his muscular arms at his sides, I could see his years in the sagging flesh of his chest and belly, but above all in his toenails. They were like turtle shells. I couldn't budge them with a heavy-duty clipper, so every three months I took him to a chiropodist for a trim. The foot doctor put a mask over his nose and mouth and sanded away as if at pieces of petrified wood.

The bath relaxed us both. While he splashed in the warm water I teased him about how good he looked after the hair washing.

"Let it grow over your ears," I suggested, "and you can be like the Beatles. There are no Yiddish rock stars, you'll have the market all to yourself."

I stretched a few white hairs to the tip of his ear. "You'll look ten years younger," I said.

"I don't wanna look younger, I wanna get dressed and make Kiddish."

After I helped him dry his back and legs, he put on the clean union suit that he carried rolled up, his socks in the middle, and placed on the back of the toilet Friday morning.

I knelt to put on his socks, then he slid his feet into sheepskin slippers at least a size too large. I held his arm as he crossed the slippery bathroom tiles, but at the safety of the dark green carpet he always broke free and hurried to his bed, where the brown suit and a clean shirt had also been waiting since morning.

Though I was the one who went out after he slept, he was the one who dressed and went to the party.

He lit the candles and prayed over the wine. When he pulled the white cover from the warm challah, he held it up to admire his work before he sang out the blessing. He waited for me to tell him how good the bread tasted. I made him wait a few seconds until I approved. Then, in a ritual no less sacred because no prayer preceded it, he grabbed the back of my neck, pulled me closer, and kissed me.

"Good Shabbes," he said. "Now eat."

Chapter 7

I started going to every peace rally I heard about, hoping to run into Debby. I had no special plan, I just wanted to see her again. Although the university had about thirty thousand students, it wasn't that hard to find someone; you saw the same faces at all the rallies. What surprised me was that I hadn't seen Debby before, probably because I'd been so holed up studying for prelims.

After our first meeting, I expected to find her the next day, just by sitting outside in the middle of campus; but I didn't see her. By the third day I even wandered into the Rainbow People's house and asked for her by name. Nobody I asked seemed to know her. There was no roster of residents, so I sat on the floor for two hours reading "Legalize Pot" brochures and old copies of the *Berkeley Barb* and once in a while sneaking in a little eighteenth-century poetry. I didn't find her. She wasn't at the coffeehouses or bookstores, either, not in the Student Union or on the grassy green area between the libraries called the DIAG, where everyone congregated at some time or other on warm summer days.

I studied in the library, and on very frequent breaks I looked for her wherever I happened to go. I knew she wouldn't come to my apartment, but I had told her that I was a teaching fellow, so I began to check my mailbox in case she decided to leave me a message on campus.

I was at that time reviewing Renaissance love poetry, which didn't help. In the poems the males were always warning the females to relent, and quickly, because age and death awaited all. A version of "Come live with me and be my love" seemed to be on every man's lips in about 1600, and with little else to fuel my daydreams Debby took over. Because I knew so little about her, I let Shakespeare and Christopher Marlowe fill in the details.

I didn't mention her again to Rocky, and he didn't ask. He liked to think his actions were final. When he ordered someone out, only an act of God could bring them back. He did, however, find me another companion.

I had been up very late studying. I was still asleep when he shook me one Thursday morning about seven-thirty.

On Monday and Thursday mornings he went to the campus synagogue. They needed ten men, and it was always a struggle to get people to come at that hour. I refused, and he didn't press me. He might still harbor pharmaceutical fantasies about me, but not theological ones. Anyway, he didn't need me. He made new friends there—most of them graduate students in philosophy whom I suspected were atheists who got up early and came to the synagogue two or three times a week to reinforce their lack of faith. That Thursday as he shook me awake, he meant to please me.

"I found someone like you," he said, and he stepped back to produce a slightly familiar face—a fellow graduate student whom I had seen but whose name I didn't know.

The thin, sandy-haired young man stood near my pillow, not certain whether he should extend a handshake to someone in underwear whose eyes were still sticky with sleep.

I rolled over, hoping they'd leave.

"Get up and talk to him," Rocky said.

"I'm tired."

"You can sleep later." When he started pulling the bedspread up, I understood that I had no chance to escape.

As soon as I stepped out of bed, Rocky had the bedspread over the pillow. The graduate student stuck out his hand. "Joel Kerner," he said. "I've seen you lots of times, but I never knew we had so much in common."

Five minutes later while Rocky poured coffee and Kerner praised the cinnamon rolls, I learned what it was we had in common.

"Your grandpa says you're having some problems understanding Shakespeare. He asked me to help."

I gave Rocky my best imitation of his own "I'll get you for this" look. It didn't bother him.

"You don't have to be ashamed," he said. "Nobody studies alone. Ask him. He knows about Shakespeare."

"I wrote my M.A. on *Antony and Cleopatra*," Kerner said modestly. "If I can help with anything . . ."

"I don't need help," I said, ignoring the guest. "If you'll leave me alone, that's plenty of help."

"Don't be so stubborn. It's no sin to ask someone who knows more."

"Excuse me," I said, "what makes you think that someone you met this morning knows more than I do?"

"Monday," Rocky corrected me. "I met him Monday, but I didn't know until today about Shakespeare. I heard him telling someone, so I brought him back."

"So anybody who knows a little about Shakespeare can help me?" Rocky nodded.

"You don't think that I know anything about Shakespeare?"

"If you did, you'd go on to something else."

I literally threw up my hands. "Do I try to tell you how to bake?"

"You don't know anything about that, either."

"What do you think I do for twelve or more hours a day?"

"That's what I've been trying to figure out," Rocky said. "You sit there, and nothing goes in. If a druggist reads something and he doesn't understand, he calls the doctor and the doctor tells him."

I looked at Kerner, who was keeping a very serious expression. "And you're the doctor?"

"M.A.," he said, "from Johns Hopkins."

"Okay," I said, "tell me about Shakespeare."

Rocky nodded and sat down to listen. "Good," he said.

Poor Kerner. He was two years behind me. His eyes blinked rapidly, and he stuttered a little. "I didn't bring any notes, I wasn't expecting . . . but if you want to discuss individual plays, I know the tragedies best."

"Okay," I said, "explain *King Lear*."

That was the kind of direct question Rocky liked.

"I don't really know what you mean by 'explain.' "

It wasn't fair to do this to Kerner, but I wanted to teach Rocky a lesson. "Just explain everything," I said, "and do it fast."

"King Lear was a foolish old man who learned the limits of his power through tragic experience. In the end he is redeemed by love."

Kerner took a big bite of cinnamon roll so he could chew for a while without having to explain more. I started to feel sorry for him. He seemed particularly humorless, but I was, too. Suddenly, watching Kerner chew and sip coffee as he thought over the explanation of *King Lear*, I burst out laughing.

"He tells you what something means and you think it's funny," Rocky said. "That's why you'll never be anything. To you laughing is more important than understanding."

"Right," I said. "King Lear was the same. You know what he did? He liked to kid around so much that he hired a professional joker to work for him—somebody who just stood around and made wisecracks. They called him a fool; he's one of the most important people in the play."

"If he was still a king," Rocky said, "then you wouldn't have to worry, you'd get that job." He looked at Kerner. "Who else did he hire, this king?"

Kerner shrugged his shoulders.

"Don't you know," I said, "that literature is an employment agency? If Hamlet had had a job, do you think he'd have had time to cause so much trouble?"

"Maybe not," Kerner said.

"And all those men in the comedies running around in the woods saying 'I love you' to this girl and then to that girl—how many of them do you think ended up going to jail for breach of promise?"

"A lot?" Kerner guessed.

"All of them," Rocky said, "every damn one. And they deserve it." He looked at me. "Remember that."

He stood and took my empty cup and Kerner's. "You see, you were mad at me, but it turns out you learned something. Does he know enough Shakespeare?"

"I think so," Kerner said.

"Good," Rocky said. "Now go learn something else."

That afternoon in the library Kerner found me. "I've been thinking about you and your grandpa all day," he said. "I've never seen anything like it."

"Him or me?" I asked.

"Both of you. But I'm really fascinated by Rocky. Would you mind if I came over again sometime? I mean, not at eight A.M."

"You wanna teach me some more?"

"No." He said, "I want to learn."

Rocky obliged him. One morning, when I came into the kitchen for breakfast, I found Kerner, literally bound in leather.

The tefillin, wooden boxes, and leather bands were all over his arm and neck. Rocky, in a hurry and assuming that Kerner had more knowledge of the procedure, had tangled the Shakespeare man in the paraphernalia of prayer. I helped untangle the acolyte. Rocky gave him a mean look.

"Seven times you wind it around your arm, and then you do this." Rocky whipped the leather band into a shape around his hand. He had been doing it every day since his own Bar Mitzvah some eighty-one years earlier. He was pretty good at it. He wouldn't slow down for Kerner.

"It's not so hard," he told Kerner, "even he learned how. Maybe he still remembers."

I did, and I demonstrated for Kerner, slowly. "Now we're even," I told Rocky. "He taught me Shakespeare and I taught him tefillin."

"Not even," Rocky said. "Shakespeare's not important, this is."

Kerner bought it. A few weeks later he was spending more time on Hebrew than on Hamlet. Though I wouldn't have chosen him as a friend, he was around so much that I did begin to like him. He was twenty-four and a seeker who had discovered his Judaism on a visit to Israel the year before. I had the feeling listening to him that had he gone to India, he would have discovered his Hinduism. It was partly the era, partly Kerner; they were a good fit. Wonders lay under every rock, especially if you had never lifted one before.

Kerner's mother died when he was six. His father and older brother raised him to become a lawyer, a businessman, a good citizen. The trip to Israel had opened his eyes, and now Rocky was opening them wider.

After the first few visits he stopped idealizing Rocky; he saw that living with him was no picnic, but he found in Rocky a human version of what drew him to Israel. He discovered an authentic Jew.

"Rocky is tough on me," he said. "He's mad all the time because I don't know enough. I see what you've been up against. Still," he said, "I'm having the time of my life."

His father insisted that Kerner finish his graduate education, but Kerner himself wanted to emigrate to Israel immediately.

"Two years," he said. "I promised my father that I'd stay two more years and that's it. Then I'm moving to Israel."

Israel, the year before, 1967, had defeated the armies of several Arab countries in the Six-Day War. The nation appeared in all its glory, every man a soldier and every soldier a hero. It was hard for anyone to resist Israel, impossible for Kerner.

While the two of them discussed religion and Zionism, I kept looking for Debby, but after a week and then two weeks and then a month, I gave up. I knew that if she was in Ann Arbor, I would have seen her. Her memory drifted away. There was, after all, little enough for me even to miss. Her robe of many colors decorated my half of the closet, and I realized that even if she had been available, I was so occupied with studying that I wouldn't have had time for her.

I did, though, make some time for the Detroit Tigers. They were in the midst of winning their first pennant in my life as a fan. Denny McLain had a shot at thirty wins, and Mickey Lolich, the left-hander, was almost as good. The televised night games were my reward for a long day of study.

Rocky usually stayed up for the first few innings. He rooted for the opposition—whoever they were. His grudge against the Tigers began when they traded Hank Greenberg, the Jewish slugger, who once hit fifty-eight home runs. He didn't mention Greenberg directly, but I understood it in all his criticisms.

"They got no power," he liked to say, "nobody to hit home runs."

It surprised me that he liked baseball. He called football "pigs rolling around in the mud" and made no attempt to learn a thing about basketball, but for baseball he even let me keep the radio on in the background.

When he'd ask the score and the Tigers were losing, he always gave me a smug look.

In the summer of 1968, I was the smug one. The Tigers were winning the pennant, and if they made it to the Series, I wouldn't have to miss a thing, my prelims would end the week before the Series.

In the world big things were happening. Robert Kennedy's assassination, the riots at the Democratic convention, Lyndon Johnson's decision not to run for reelection, and above all the continuing and ever-escalating war. I did not shut my eyes to the news; Rocky wouldn't let me. His friend Walter Cronkite told us the way it was each day, but I was so immersed in my reading, so full of the life of the past, that the events of the day seemed no more immediate than the 1666 fire of London.

Although I tried to insulate myself from what was happening around me, the Defense Department broke through my barrier of books. In the mail came greetings from my draft board. I showed Rocky the letter because I knew that on this issue he'd be on my side. Although I was against the war, I hadn't burned my draft card—and I didn't consider going to Canada or anywhere else. With all my antiwar beliefs, when it came down to it, I sometimes felt like a traitor. I knew I was right, but being right wasn't enough.

Rocky and I each tried to figure a way out. I went to the graduate dean, who told me that there was no problem, all graduate students in good standing received automatic deferments. I didn't have to choose between serving my country or my conscience. I just had to stay in school, as I planned.

Rocky and my mother had their own plan. They contacted a dermatologist in Grand Rapids who had treated me for acne when I was sixteen. Her office was in her house. I never saw another patient there. She was almost as old as Rocky. When I had an appointment I rang the bell, pounded on her door, and then waited on the porch, hoping her hearing aid was on.

She had treated Rocky in the 1930s for a burn. She was eighty-three when I was in high school and told me she still had acne outbreaks whenever she drank a Coke. Rocky went with me and always baked something for her. I sat in her living room, and she shined a flashlight on my face. She told me to wash with Dial soap and stay away from Coke and chocolate.

She charged five dollars. I hadn't seen her for a decade. Rocky took the bus to Grand Rapids and returned that same night. He carried a letter from the dermatologist.

"If he goes into the army," Dr. Herrick wrote, "Max is likely to develop pustular acne. I don't think he should be drafted."

Rocky watched my expression as I read. "She's an important doctor," he said. "They'll listen to her."

"Do you think the army cares if I get pimples?"

"You think they wanna pay doctor bills? Just show them this letter," he said. "The army will know what to do."

Chapter 8

*T*he warmth I felt against my knee surprised me. I had heard the scraping sound, but who expects a dog in the general reading room? It was the day before the prelims, and I was more than ready. I was daydreaming about the World Series, so when I felt the dog's tail and bent down to see him busy, engaged with getting the gum that someone, probably years earlier, had stuck under the table, I was more amused than distracted. But others were more disturbed, so I grabbed him by the collar and led him downstairs and out the front door. I watched him sniff the air, look around among the guitar players and Frisbee throwers and walkers and bicyclers on the DIAG. I watched him run right to a girl in a brown sack dress. He jumped up to lick her face. She laughed as he almost knocked her down.

I ran almost as fast as he did. She had both temple pieces on her glasses now.

"Remember me?" I said.

"Oh, yeah," she said. "The guy with the friendly roommate." There were hundreds of people around and her dog was barking at me for getting the attention he wanted and there was someone standing next to her, talking to her, but I only noticed her.

"I looked everywhere for you."

"I've been gone," she said. "I had to stay home the rest of the summer."

All the Renaissance admonitions about time had influenced me. I didn't waste any.

"I missed you," I said. "Give me another chance?"

The person she was talking to, a dark-skinned man in a suit, coughed. "Excuse me," he said, "we were talking."

"This is Bijan," Debby said, "he's from Iran."

I stepped back. "I'm sorry to interrupt," I said, but I didn't go away.

"Let's go have coffee," Bijan said. He took her arm.

"I'm sorry that I was so rude," I said to Bijan. "I know I'm barging in, but I've been looking for her. I can't let her get away without knowing where she lives."

Debby borrowed a card from him—with the gold crest of the Iranian National Oil Company. On the back she wrote her address and phone number. The two of them and the dog walked across campus. I stood there watching.

They were almost at the corner of State Street where the campus green ended and the stores began. A group of Hare Krishnas was singing only a few feet from me. I watched in the distance as Bijan crossed the busy commercial street. Debby and the dog turned back to campus. The dog got to me first and slobbered my cheeks, Debby came running and called him off.

"How'd you know I was waiting?" I asked.

"I didn't," she said. "I was just hoping."

She had coffee with me instead of the foreign student, and I learned that she'd had a run-in with her mother, not at all an unusual event— that her parents had taken away her car and demanded that she stop being a hippie.

"Did you?" I asked.

"Of course," she said. "I joined the DAR and had my nails done." She held them up. "I'm not kidding. Look."

I could still see bits of frosted pink polish. For the first time I noticed her squished thumbnail, as strange as Popeye's forearm. It was half the size of her other nails, round and silly like a clown on her beautiful hand.

"My odd thumb," she said.

"From sucking?" I asked.

"From nothing," she said, "like my other defects."

"It's not a defect."

I held her thumb, examined it, and then brought it to my lips. "Tasty nailpolish."

"Frosted lemon. I did join the DAR, too, only I used the name Tricia Nixon. My mother was so impressed that she allowed me to return to Ann Arbor under the condition that I do nothing to stop the war or help the poor. I am only to study."

"Boring. That's all I've been doing," I said, "since the time I saw you."

"But you have such an exciting home life. When it's his turn, does he cruise the old age homes and then you get to throw the ladies out? No kidding. Do you go through this a lot?"

"You're the first. I hope it doesn't start a streak."

She loved it when I told her about breach of promise.

"He's a gentleman after all. I like that. So if I ever do go back there you have to marry me—right?"

"Let me pass prelims first, then we'll discuss it."

We were in a dark green booth in a restaurant called Drake's. In her loose-fitting brown dress and expensive sandals she seemed so unlike the barefoot girl in ragged jeans. Yet even dressed like a sorority girl, she looked like a waif. Her sad brown eyes filled with pleasure when I held her hand. We discovered that we were both from Grand Rapids, not such a rare coincidence, but I was willing to read it as a good sign. Through the glass window her dog, George, watched every move. He couldn't take his eyes off her. Neither could I.

On the day of my first exam Rocky pulled out his king-size thermos bottle and had it ready for me at the door. It was probably made in the thirties, real glass and a stainless-steel cup. He took it to work every day and used to let me sip from the cup after he'd added extra milk. When I saw the bottle at the door, it was the first time I knew that he took me seriously about all this studying. I realized that Kerner had probably gotten through to him.

He couldn't have given me a better gift. I never opened it, but having that thermos bottle on the table in front of me was the best lucky charm I could have received. I used it all week, with the original coffee.

I didn't see Debby that week, but every night after each of the four prelims, I talked to her. We had a date for the upcoming Saturday night, then on Sunday I wanted her to watch the Series opener with me. She wasn't sure, she said, she wasn't much of a baseball fan. I was a little worried about where we'd watch. I was planning to stay home and watch it with Rocky, but if she accepted, I'd already selected a bar as an alternative.

I had a note in the mail from Kerner wishing me luck. I appreciated it. It turned out he was the one who needed it.

I knew something was wrong when Rocky came home from the synagogue on Saturday and didn't immediately yell at me because I was still in bed. I had finished on Friday and was treating myself to a sleep-in morning, but I didn't expect such quiet approval from him. When he didn't come in to make the bed, I worried and went out to the kitchen.

He was taking out some dishes.

"We said Tehlilim for Kerner," Rocky said. "They say he won't live through the day." That was all he knew.

I started making telephone calls, but nobody knew anything. The hospital operator wouldn't tell me if Kerner was a patient, but a few minutes after noon I did get a call from an intensive care nurse.

"Mr. Kerner asked me to call you," she said. "Could you please come over quickly?"

She told me he had been shot the night before in front of the library as he was walking home. The bullet had entered his neck at the third vertebra. He was stable and awaiting neurosurgery. His family was on the way.

"He asked for you," the nurse said. "He wants you to pray with him."

"Is he going to live?" I asked.

"Get here as quickly as you can," she said.

The war, which I had tried to avoid all summer as I studied, had made an unscheduled appearance. On the diagonal where Debby's dog and a dozen others chased Frisbees, where lovers held hands and Hare Krishnas chanted, right there beneath floating peace banners and in view of a dozen or so bystanders, Kerner, his mind probably on Zion, had walked past an angry drunk.

The man had been standing in front of the library for an hour, harassing several passersby. Nobody took him seriously. Crazy people stopped you all the time. Some of them weren't even crazy. This one was.

A corporal who ran out on his unit—AWOL. A soldier with a gun and training. How free and easy the students must have seemed to him that night—carrying books, laughing, not even noticing him until he yelled and shoved a few, and even then they just walked away from him. Kerner had tried to walk away, too, and succeeded until a U.S. Army bullet manufactured to bring sorrow to the enemy delivered it instead directly into the spine of my friend.

The nurse was waiting for me. She took me right to him where he lay in a tiny room off the large intensive care unit.

"We're getting him ready for surgery," she said, "but he wants to see you. Please hurry." She stood next to me. "Don't touch him," she said. "We don't want the slightest movement."

I waved to him—I didn't know yet that he couldn't wave back. I had to bend down close to his lips to hear his voice. His face looked good. There was a small bruise on his forehead. That was all. I believed the nurse, but I also wouldn't have been surprised to see him stand and walk away from the medical machinery that surrounded him.

"Help me say the Shma," he said.

I opened the prayer book I had brought along and read aloud the Hebrew creed—which, though said at other times, too, is what believers utter with their last breath.

Since I didn't know what else to say, I just kept reading the words one after another, far more than any dying person could utter without such prompting. When the nurse tapped my shoulder and the surgical team wheeled him away, we were about at the end of the paragraph telling the Jews to wear tefillin between their eyes and put signs upon their doorposts.

I went home and told Rocky all that I knew. I omitted just one thing. Before I left the nurse told me that the spinal column had been cut. If Kerner survived, he'd never again have use of his arms or legs.

Rocky prayed for him from one of the oversize books that he'd brought with him from Lithuania. The bindings had broken many times, and he'd repaired them with Scotch tape and masking tape and big chunks of black electrical tape. Whenever I glanced into the books, those frayed yellowing pages looked just as messy to my eye as the homemade bindings.

At five Kerner's father and older brother called. They didn't know anyone in Ann Arbor. The nurse told them that Joel had called me. They were in the surgical waiting room. I telephoned Debby. She wasn't home. I left a message canceling our date and drove to the hospital.

His father, his brother, and I waited until the surgeon came out at about eight-thirty. The news was as good as it could be. He would be able to breathe, the bullet had not touched the second vertebra. "He should be able to move his neck, too," the doctor said.

"What else?" Kerner senior asked.

"Everything above the neck—his eyes, his face."

I couldn't look at his father when he heard. I excused myself. I didn't know whether to pray for his recovery or not. My mind was a strange combination, anger and sorrow over what was happening to Kerner and all those facts of literary history still sitting there fresh and absolutely trivial.

As I walked down the steps of the University Hospital, George ran up to greet me. On a bench beneath a lamppost, Debby waited.

"How'd you know?" I asked.

"You left a message, and then I heard it on the news. By now everyone knows. They already caught the guy who did it."

She put her arms around me. "I'm sorry," she said, "I really am."

The Tigers beat St. Louis in seven games. I caught only fragments of the action. Instead I spent most of that week looking at a little screen in the intensive care unit that recorded Kerner's heartbeats. Every day he got stronger. When the doctors told him he would be a quadriplegic, he surprised everyone. He still wanted to live.

Once Kerner was well enough to move to a ward he wanted to study, but the staff was not pleased. There were sixteen people on the ward; a few had use of their arms, none had use of their legs. Visiting hours ended at seven because the nurses had so much to do. They enforced the early hours even though it inconvenienced lots of families.

"Nobody's here for a short stay," Helen, the head nurse, explained to me. She had worked on that ward for a decade. She was brisk and efficient. Nobody argued with her. "They can learn to work around the hours, so can you."

When Kerner told the neurosurgeon he wanted to study for his prelims and needed someone to read to him, the doctor got him special permission. Each evening from seven to nine someone could read to him. Everyone in the English department volunteered, but after a few days Helen called a halt.

"They're not studying, they're visiting." She sent one of the volunteers home early. Kerner was about to lose his extra visiting privilege when he worked out a compromise. He could have someone help him study from seven to nine, but it had to be the same person every day. That, Helen said, would avoid the temptation to do more than study.

Kerner asked for me again. We developed a regular routine. I came home earlier to have dinner with Rocky. Rocky baked something for Kerner and sent it with me. I picked up Debby at quarter to seven.

While I read to Kerner on the eighth-floor ward, Debby studied in the hospital cafeteria and George waited for both of us at the bus stop out front.

Rocky visited Kerner from time to time, though by mutual agreement they put off the Hebrew study temporarily.

Debby and I didn't go to many movies and never had time for bars or parties. Sometimes after the hospital we stopped at the library. Then, as quickly as we could, we went to her apartment.

In February, the man who shot Kerner was sentenced—three to five years.

Chapter 9

R ocky knew something was up. He noticed that I didn't come home sometimes until one or two or even later, although none of his realizations stopped him from waking me at seven. Getting me out of bed was one of his main jobs, like setting me up in a career and making sure I followed the straight-and-narrow path.

No matter how tired, I had to get out of bed, eat oatmeal and a roll, take my herring or smoked fish or boiled chicken lunch, and hurry out of the apartment. Sometimes I managed to get in a few hours at the library before I collapsed, others days I didn't even try. I just went right to Debby's apartment and slept until ten or eleven.

Debby didn't understand why I put up with it. Filial affection was not her strong point. When I met her mother I understood why.

Harriet was alone when she walked into Debby's apartment. She took two steps onto the cracked linoleum and stopped abruptly as if to await a bellhop who would be appearing in a few seconds with her bags. She looked around the living room/dining room/kitchen, taking in everything slowly, as if checking for termites or the early signs of water leakage from the pipes. I stood in front of the three-legged couch, near the books that supported the load of the missing leg. Her eyes passed me by as if I were a sign at a bus stop.

Debby had told me that her mother was almost fifty, but her figure had remained girlish, and even her face, aided by light makeup, had aged without losing its beauty. She had bleached hair and wore an off white linen suit that would show spots if she sat down anywhere in the apartment. She demonstrated no inclination to sit. After her visual scan she walked quickly into the bedroom, then turned her eyes from the bathroom as if she couldn't stand anymore. Debby said nothing. Since neither mother nor daughter greeted one another, I stood silently, too, waiting for one of them to begin. Harriet finally broke the ice.

"Why didn't you tell me it's a basement?" she said. "Rats live in basements."

She nodded to me as she walked past as if I were the doorman. Debby didn't let her get away with it.

"Hello, Mother," Debby said. "This is the person I told you about. You could at least be civil enough to greet him."

Harriet extended her fingertips to me and pulled them away from my sweaty grip as fast as she could.

Nothing satisfied her. The refrigerator motor was too loud. The faucets leaked and didn't have enough water pressure. The mattress was soft, the linoleum filthy.

Finally Debby stopped her. "Did the housing bureau send you?" she asked. "Or is this a friendly visit?"

"Everything I do is friendly," Harriet said. She was in the process of opening all the closets. "And where are your things?" she asked me.

"At my house," I said. "You don't think I'd live in a place like this, do you?"

From the kitchen Debby bit her cheeks to keep from laughing and gave me the V-sign with her fingers.

"What do you study?" Harriet asked.

"Literature."

"Is that practical?"

With a look, Debby encouraged me to take her on.

"Of course," I said. "Some of the most successful people can read and write."

She chose to ignore me. She dusted the couch first with a tissue, then changed her mind about sitting there. She pulled out her checkbook and wrote six separate postdated checks as she stood.

"This is for the rent."

"So you approve after all," Debby said.

"No," she answered, "but you signed a lease, and I believe that a promise is binding. I hope you remember the promises you made."

"Of course I do," Debby said. She looked at me. "Have I done anything to stop the war?" she asked. I shook my head. "And if you don't believe him, just keep watching the news. The bombing, the napalming, it's right on schedule."

"I'm sure my daughter has convinced you that I'm a warmonger," Harriet said. "She doesn't believe that I want peace as much as any of you, but I want peace in the family, too, not just in Vietnam. I don't want my daughter getting arrested every two weeks."

"C'mon, Ma," Debby said, "where else am I gonna meet such interesting guys?"

Harriet looked at me as if to decide in one glance whether I really might be interesting. While she looked me over I asked if she'd like coffee or soda.

"No, thank you," she said, "but if Debby will change her clothes, I'll be happy to take both of you to lunch."

Debby had dressed in preparation. She wore a white blouse and a flowing Indian skirt and had even put on a little eye makeup.

"What would you like me to wear?" Debby asked.

"A bra," Harriet said, "and a slip if you insist on wearing that see-through skirt."

Debby went to the bedroom and returned quickly, wearing jeans and a V-neck T-shirt to emphasize the missing bra.

"All right," Harriet said, "wear what you had on. Give me those jeans so I can throw them in the trash on the way out."

Debby changed back to her original outfit, and they both seemed satisfied, as if they could relax now that they'd had the necessary face-off. In the suburban restaurant Harriet seemed almost pleasant.

"I know I'm in the attack mode," she said. "Debby brings it out. She always has. If you like her, you have me to thank. She has fashioned herself to be my exact opposite, and I think she's succeeded."

"Yes," Debby said, "but it's a constant struggle. I have to fight the impulse to have my hair washed on Mondays, Wednesdays, and Fridays. And those sunny days when I could be on the golf course instead of sitting in a class or in my rat-infested apartment . . ."

Harriet had already downed a glass of wine, which seemed to help. She even laughed. "I didn't say it was rat-infested."

"She didn't," I added, happy to agree with Harriet about something. She ignored me completely.

During lunch Debby didn't talk back. Neither did I. After Harriet paid, she pulled two credit cards out of her wallet and handed them to Debby.

"Saks," she said, "and Jacobsen's, I didn't know they had a store here. Ann Arbor has finally improved a little."

Debby accepted the cards.

"Use them," Harriet said.

That night when we were lying in bed reading, Debby opened the drawer of her bedside table and threw the cards in. There were at least a dozen others already there.

"Do you ever use any of them?"

"No," Debby said, "she'd get too much satisfaction. Her aim is to have me spend and then to hold it over my head for control. If you don't do this, then I take away Exxon or Saks or the car or college."

"I used to envy the rich. You're making me change my opinions."

"I'm not rich," Debby said, "she is. Remember we're opposites."

It was true that Debby seemed to have less spending money than I did, and she never bought anything except food and toiletries, but I could tell that she didn't understand money. In the supermarket she paid no attention to the prices. She didn't balance her checkbook. She never gave a thought to calling friends across the country and talking as long as she liked.

They were little things, but the very fact that I noticed them bothered me.

Partly I think to convince me that she was serious about breaking away from her parents' financial domination, Debby got a job. She supervised the playground during lunch for children in nursery school and after three for the older children who stayed late.

When I could, I joined her on the playground. I loved the way the fourth-graders yelled "He's up!" when I grabbed a bat and moved back almost against the wire fence barely a hundred feet away.

If Debby was pitching, as she often did, she didn't make it easy. She could throw the ball at least as well as I could, and when I came to the plate she switched from underhand to sidearm. She played for the girls and I for the boys. The fourth-graders inspired us with the intensity of their continuous duel. The boys had always won until Debby showed up; now the nine-year-old males counted on me to return them to constant victory.

I wore my Tigers cap, the same one I'd bought on my first trip to Briggs Stadium. I'd kept it for years as a souvenir, and now that the dark blue had faded and the famous ornate *D* was losing its glue, I wore it to keep the sun out of my eyes as the pitcher stared in at me.

Debby was a half inch shorter than I and about the same weight, but more agile. She moved effortlessly. I noticed it not only when she pitched, but when she swam or jogged or threw a stick for George to fetch. She wasted no movements.

When she pitched, she kept her hair in a short ponytail that stuck out of the back of her baseball cap, a light brown one that bore the logo of her father's factory.

She didn't hesitate to brush me back from the plate.

"Ready, Mr. Rotten Apple?" she liked to ask. Once she said it, the girls took up the chant: "Mr. Rotten Apple, Mr. Rotten Apple. . . ."

When my team tried to rile her they yelled, "We want a pitcher, not a belly itcher." The more they yelled, the more she taunted the boys by scratching her stomach before she turned to lob one down the middle to them.

———————

Writing a dissertation followed by lots of fun on the playground by day, reading to Kerner in the evening, and going to Debby's apartment at night, I found that my life took on a new fullness. Someone was left out.

He never said anything; I didn't even see him reading the want ads. When I felt guilty for spending less time at the apartment, I told myself he was probably happy because I was working so hard. I didn't try to incorporate him into the life I was living, the life in which Debby, not Rocky, was now at the center.

I still came back to the apartment for dinner every day, but I didn't stay for the news, and sometimes I hurried away, even forgetting his midweek bath. His life hadn't changed, mine had somersaulted.

Though I hated to bring him up, I told Debby one evening how guilty I felt for leaving him alone so much of the time.

"Guilty," she said. "My God, you set the clock for three—you crawl out of my bed and drive across town so that he can wake you up at seven, and you feel guilty toward him. What about me—how do you think I feel at three when you tiptoe out to 'Grampa'?"

"You've got other things in your life," I said. "He doesn't."

"You told me he likes to watch baseball."

"With me. He likes to watch with me, not alone."

"There must be something else you can find for him to do. What about the synagogue?"

"He already goes there every hour it's open. That's not enough for him."

"What about a hobby?"

"He doesn't have hobbies—people like him only understand work. He wouldn't know what a hobby is."

"Don't be so sure," Debby said. "I think you're his hobby, a full-time one."

She laughed at my herring and sardine and boiled chicken lunches. She didn't even let me put them in her refrigerator. I kept waiting for her to mention meeting him again, but I was relieved that she seemed happy to put it off.

I didn't tell Debby that I wanted to marry her, I told Kerner. He had amazed the medical staff by going at his graduate work a month after being shot. They thought he was the most dedicated student on earth. I knew better. Helen, the head nurse, had been right to suspect us. We only talked literature when we had to. Whenever a nurse was suspicious, Kerner, who knew a lot of poetry by heart, would break into quotation. When Helen was on duty we had to be extra careful; sometimes she actually stood at the foot of the bed to listen.

" 'Had we but world enough, and time,' " Kerner said to her, " 'This

coyness, Lady, were no crime. We would sit down, and think which way
To walk, and pass our long love's day.' "

"I know you're visiting," she said.

"We have to talk," I said. "We can't just quote poetry for two
hours."

In the midst of all the suffering on that ward, Kerner and I managed
to become close friends. When Helen wasn't there we talked openly. "I
don't want to be an English teacher," he said. "I never did. I'm just going
through the motions. Whether or not I get a Ph.D. didn't matter before,
now what difference can it make?"

"It will help you get a job."

"Getting a job," he said, "will be the least of my problems. What
about you? What will you do when you finish?"

When I told him I wanted to marry Debby, he had only one question.

"What will Rocky do? Will he still live with you?"

"I don't know," I said. "He could go back to Grand Rapids, but the
synagogue isn't Orthodox anymore, and all his friends are dead. He'd
just be waiting to die, he'd have nothing to look forward to."

"What about Israel?" Kerner asked.

"Be serious."

"I am serious. I'm going, why can't he?"

"I want him a little closer than that."

"What about Debby?"

I tried not to answer. I looked around to see if Helen was nearby.

"It's hard for you, isn't it?" he asked.

"I feel ridiculous complaining to you when you hardly complain."

"I can't do anything about being paralyzed," he said, "but you can
get unstuck. Do you and Debby talk about it?"

"I don't mention him unless I have to. He's not number one on her
list. But I'll have to think of something."

Rocky had been thinking, too, and he made the first move. Instead
of looking for a job, he decided to find a new place to live.

"I've been looking," he told me one night as we hurried through a
dinner of cottage cheese and canned peaches. "You got no time to keep
running out here to me. And you're never home. It's a waste of money.
I don't need such a big apartment."

His solution—we'd split up—he'd get a single room on campus, and so would I. It was a more elegant plan than any I'd thought of.

"When will I see you?" I asked.

"At the synagogue," he said, a biting answer since I went only on Saturday, not to the daily minyan as he did.

"And where else?"

"Wherever you want," he said. "You're the one that's busy, not me."

I wasn't sure he'd carry out this plan. I thought he was merely using the suggestion to remind me to spend more time with him. I admired his subtlety and determined to make more time for him.

I was wrong. He meant it, and looking for a room put him in such a great mood that I didn't protest. Finally he had a job—something to do every day. He rode into campus with me in the morning and began walking along the residential streets where the old Victorian houses were mingled with ugly modern two- and three-story apartment houses stuck together by investors to lease to students—three rooms as expensively as possible.

In the old houses you could sometimes get a bargain. Undergraduates didn't want single rooms, they liked company and the security of a dorm—TVs and study halls and even the regularity of the food they complained about. In a single room you really were on your own for everything.

As I thought about it, the room might not be so bad. He'd be on campus in the middle of things. He could walk to rallies, even sit in on classes if he ever wanted to. Instead of seeing him at seven A.M. and briefly for dinner, I could pick other times, maybe four to six every day. It might work. Best of all, it would free me to move in with Debby. She had offered.

"If you ever get sick of the suburbs," she said, "there really is room in my closet."

I already kept a few shirts and trousers there—not moving in would be silly. She didn't hide our living together—I did.

The idea of being out on his own in the middle of campus excited Rocky. "If you can become a doctor of something," he said, "everybody can. Maybe I will, too."

"No," I said, "if you study for anything, it's gonna be druggist."

"It's no joke," he said. "If I had my own store, I'd still be working, but I'm too old for that."

"All right," I said, "become a philosopher and just sit around all day like I do. Nobody's too old to sit around and do this." I made my underlining gesture.

"I know you're working," he said. "I see how tired you are. You don't eat enough, either. You're too skinny—you're probably not finishing lunch."

"Maybe you should start baking some cookies to fatten me up."

"You want cookies," he said, "go ask Betty Crocker, not me."

"Maybe I'm losing weight because of your bread."

"Nothing's wrong with the bread."

"I don't know," I said. "Some days the rye bread tastes like it needs more sugar."

"Dummy," he said, "it's a sour dough. You stay with the books and I'll make the bread. But I'm gonna give you two boiled eggs in the lunches."

"I can't eat so much."

"You'll eat them later for a snack."

Hard-boiled I might have, but Rocky insisted on soft three-minute eggs. He ate one every morning—making a hole on the top and scooping out the contents with a teaspoon. I couldn't see myself doing that on the steps of the library or in the Student Union where Debby and I usually ate.

He was convinced that hard-boiled eggs were bad for you but soft-boiled were not. I didn't try to change his mind. I just gave the eggs to George. In a few weeks the cholesterol made his coat glow.

Looking for a room occupied Rocky and relieved me, until he walked past the Burns Park Elementary School. It never occurred to me that he'd stray to that neighborhood, completely residential, but he was on his way to answer an ad in the *Michigan Daily* that offered a garage apartment in return for lawn care and general handyman work. I can imagine what the couple, expecting a student, thought when Rocky rang their doorbell.

It must have been especially disappointing to him because he was in a foul mood when he walked past the schoolyard. I didn't see him approaching from behind home plate.

I held the bat in my hand. The outfield was deep, and there were boys on base. Debby glared at me, took off her cap to wipe her brow. I waved the bat. The kids loved it when we went through the big league motions. She ran her hand through her fine brown hair, which hung straight and then curved just below her ears. Half-inch bangs slipped down her forehead. She tanned easily and was already nut brown even in early spring. She turned her back to check the outfield. She rubbed up the tattered softball, pounded her glove, eyed the plate, gave me a mean look, wrinkled her nose. Ruthie Hankins, her catcher, gave her the sign, the fist against the glove. I knocked the end of the flattened milk carton that served as home plate.

"Put it here, belly itcher!" I yelled. She itched her belly, and my boys let her have it: "Belly itcher, belly itcher . . ."

She came in with a high fast one. I swung and missed, and not on purpose. I struck out. The girls were going wild, mobbing Debby, the boys, holding mitts that were too big for them, were already thinking about next time.

"Lazy son of a beetch." I heard the gruff whisper. His face was against the chain-link fence. He scared the children standing nearby.

"This is how you're working."

Debby freed herself from the girls and walked to the fence. "Hi," she said, "you want a turn at bat?"

Rocky spit and literally ran from the park.

I waited until dinnertime, then drove home. There was no meal, and he had already packed the duffel bag that I'd bought for him when he moved to Ann Arbor.

"If you'd listen," I said, "I could explain."

"You listen," he said. "I got a new place."

"All right," I said, "but there's something more important. I don't want to hide this from you any longer. I have a girlfriend."

"So does every dog on the street," he said.

"So I'm a dog on the street because I play softball for an hour with some kids."

"You're no good," he said, "that's all. After tomorrow you won't see me."

"I'd be just as happy as you if that were possible, but it's not, so sit down and talk to me."

"Go talk to her," he said. "Go bring in her clothes."

"I'm not kicking you out. There's room for both of you."

"If I wanted to live in a whorehouse," he said, "I could have stayed in Grand Rapids. They've got 'em there, too."

He went to his room and slammed the door. I called Debby to tell her that I was going to stay home that night.

"He has a tantrum, spits at me, and you reward him by baby-sitting him. Just what he wants."

"Lay off," I said. "He's moving out tomorrow. I want to spend his last night here with him. I'm sorry he spit at you. I apologize for him— what more can I do?"

I didn't sleep that night, and neither did Rocky. I heard him opening and closing drawers. At three he went to the kitchen to boil water and was in the bathroom when the kettle started to whistle. I ran out to stop it before the howl woke the neighbors. He came out of the bathroom and drank his usual breakfast liquid—hot water into which he squeezed half a lemon. I sat across from him, drinking instant coffee.

"Go back to sleep," he said.

"If you go back to sleep," I said, "then I will."

"To me, it's morning," he said. "I got to pack."

He didn't have to wake me at seven. I was lying on the couch just waiting for the "Today" show to begin so I could turn on the TV. His duffel bag sat against the door. He had tied his favorite shoes, brown-and-white wingtips, around the canvas handle to keep them from being crushed. Instead of shoe trees, wadded newspapers helped the shoes keep their shape.

He was dressed for the move in his brown double-breasted suit that was much older than I was. His red tie had so many egg yolk stains that they seemed to be part of the design. His white hair was combed, and he wore a dark brown tweed cap almost the color of his suit.

Only the blue Adidas running shoes that I had bought him kept him from looking like a distinguished retired executive.

He looked confident, and he was. He had the kind of confidence that a second-guesser can never have. At 7:05 A.M. he was out the door, pulling the heavy bag down the hallway.

I hurried out to help him load it into the car. He sat on the backseat like a passenger in a taxi and kept silent.

Usually he sat next to me and told me every time I chose one direction over another that I was going the wrong way. We sat in the car. I didn't start the engine. Finally he broke the ice.

"C'mon," he said, "or I'm going to the bus."

"I'll go," I said, "when you tell me where."

He reached into his trouser pocket and handed me an address written on the back flap of an envelope. His new address was 16 Vaughn Street. The return address on the envelope was Taiwan.

I had no trouble finding the street. It was around the corner from Debby's apartment. I carried his bag up the porch steps and into the entryway of the old three-story Georgian mansion that had probably housed some distinguished professor and his family during World War I while Rocky was learning English in night school. He walked behind me, so aloof and formal that I wouldn't have been surprised if he had tipped me.

"Where?" I asked.

He pointed to a room to the left of the staircase, took a key out of his zippered change purse, and tried to unlock the door. From the kitchen four Chinese men, their faces close to their steaming bowls of rice, put down their chopsticks to stare at us. I had been up for so long that I thought they were having lunch, not breakfast.

He couldn't get the door open. One of the men who seemed to be my age or older rose to help. His English was halting.

"Excuse," he said, "I assist."

I introduced myself. Rocky didn't. Once the door opened he dragged in the duffel bag. There was an iron frame bed and a chair. That was it. No desk, no lamp, no table, no dresser. I looked around for a closet—none. The room itself probably had been a closet. Someone cut a tiny window into it, and presto, Rocky had a new home. The whole thing was about three times the length of his duffel bag.

The man who helped us with the bag, Richard Huang, seemed embarrassed by the inadequacies of the room.

"Small," he said, "but maybe very comfortable."

Rocky had already put his two-tone shoes under the bed. He unzipped his bag and held a handful of socks and underwear. He walked around looking for a place to put them. Finally he laid them on the bed. Then he stopped.

"You can go," he told me, "I'm all set."

He almost pushed me as he closed the door. I stood in the hallway
with Richard Huang. The three men in the kitchen who had gone back
to their meal looked up again to contemplate me. Richard invited me to
the kitchen to join them. They fit me in around the small table. Someone
handed me a bowl and chopsticks. Only Richard and one other man
spoke much English. They were lab assistants and math grad students
who were hoping to learn English. The landlord had sublet Rocky's room
when one of their colleagues, too frustrated with English, went back to
Taiwan. Everyone in the house was Chinese.

"He student?" Richard asked me.

"No," I said, "he's my grandfather."

"Small room," Richard said.

"Small room," I echoed.

I kept my eye on Rocky's door and wondered if the lab assistant had
come home only to sleep.

Although Richard Huang knew limited English, I think he understood some of what Rocky was not saying—the angry looks, the way he
closed the door on me, those were universal gestures.

"Grandpa angry?" he said.

"Yes," I answered.

"Because room too small?"

"No—he's angry at me—because I have a girlfriend."

I spoke loud, as if that would make me easier to understand, but in
a sentence I had told Richard exactly the problem.

"Very sorry," he said, "what is that?"

The lab assistants finished their breakfast. One of them washed the
bowls and sticks, then put the remaining rice into the refrigerator, though
not before asking me again, in signs, if I wanted more to eat. I thanked
him. By eight they had all gone off to work. I knew that Debby, around
the corner, had just stepped out of the shower and was wrapping a big
white towel around her hair to squeeze the water out before she rubbed
her scalp vigorously for a minute, then slipped on blue jeans and a
T-shirt. Sometimes on her way out the door for a nine o'clock history
class she would snatch a bite of one of Rocky's cinnamon rolls that I
brought over. Grudgingly she admitted they weren't bad, but she preferred Sara Lee.

I dozed off at the kitchen table, but I heard him when he opened his door and then several others, looking for the bathroom. There wasn't one on the first floor. He had to trudge upstairs. Before I heard him flush the toilet, I peeked into his room. He had put everything back into the duffel bag. The two-tone shoes were tied around the handle again.

He walked outside and onto the driveway. I wasn't spying, just sitting in the kitchen. I wanted him to see me, but he didn't look up. He opened the wooden garage and looked around among crates, old tires, and filing cabinets until he found what he was looking for—the galvanized garbage can. He checked to make sure the lid fit tightly, then he pulled it closer to the door and closed the garage. When he walked to the corner I was afraid he might see Debby, but it was already after nine. Unless she'd overslept I was safe.

I put my head on the kitchen table and slept until I heard a door slam. It was ten-fifteen. I washed my face with cold water at the kitchen sink to wake myself and dried it on a paper towel. At ten-thirty I knocked on his door. He opened it.

"I thought you were one of the Chinese guys," he said.

"They're all at work," I said, "won't be home until five or six or later."

"Good," he said, "I don't need 'em."

"How much are you paying?" I asked.

"Twenty a week," he said.

I gave a pained expression. "Twenty a week, what the hell do you think this is, a hotel? For twenty a week you can get a private bath and a kitchen. The landlord took you."

"The son of a beetch knew I was desperate," he said.

"You told him you needed it right away?"

He nodded.

"You were on the way back from the playground?"

He gave me an angry look, but he nodded again.

"You're lucky he didn't say twenty-five. You'd have paid that, too, wouldn't you?"

"It's as hard to find a room as a job here," he said. "They get you coming and going."

"Did you sign a lease?"

"No," he said.

"How much did you give him?"

"Two weeks in advance," Rocky said. "Forty bucks."

"If you let me, I'll write the guy a letter on university stationery and tell him he has to give you back your money. I'll tell him there's housing codes. Every room has got to have a closet."

"Tell him," Rocky said, "to lower the rent for the Chinese guys, too. They don't know the laws—he's probably taking everyone."

"Nobody should rent from such a person," I said.

I already had my hand on his duffel bag. He didn't stop me.

"I'll get your money back."

"You can keep half," he said. "A lawyer would charge that much, too."

Chapter 10

*H*e moved back, but it wasn't over. He had made up his mind to leave. After the rooming house fiasco he really bit the bullet. That afternoon, when I expected a reprieve, he handed me a slip of paper from his wallet. I had no idea how long he'd been carrying it around—the address of the Jewish Home for the Aged in Detroit.

"Give me a break," I said. "Relax for a while before you move out again."

"I'm not relaxing," he said, "until I get out from here."

He dictated:

Dear Head of the Home,

    I'd like a room there. I'm independent. I get $120 Social Security every month. I'm right now living with my grandson in Ann Arbor, which is close. I can be there in an hour if he takes me or maybe two or three hours by bus. What street is the closest bus stop?

    My brother used to own a bakery on Livernois Avenue so I

know Detroit. Call me at my grandson's to tell me when I should come there.

Then he'd signed the page with his florid "Herman Goodstein."

I folded his letter and put a different one in the envelope. "Please send me an application for admission," I wrote, then I copied his signature. I didn't mail it. The letter sat on my desk. When he talked about a room on campus I thought it might have worked, at least for a while. I could have checked on him every day, and it would be a matter that was just between us and a landlord. But a home was something else—a bureaucracy with all sorts of procedures and rules. I knew he would hate the home and probably try to leave within a week or maybe a day.

"What'll you do," I asked him, "if they let you into the home and then you want to leave?"

"I'll leave," he said.

"Where will you go?"

"That's not your worry."

"It's not my worry," I said, "but I'll have to forward your mail. What if the Social Security check comes to me, or your life insurance bill?"

"I'll let you know where to send everything."

"You sure you want to try the home?"

"I told you I'm going," he said. "Every day I'll check the mail."

When I understood that he was not going to let it drop, I mailed the letter, no more certain than he was where it would lead us.

Debby laughed when I told her about the boarding house. "You should have left him there for a week or so," she said, "to teach him a lesson."

"I couldn't do that to the Chinese guys," I said. "They were too nice."

She didn't storm around the way Rocky did, but in her own way, Debby was also putting me through a test. We all knew that this threesome wasn't going to last, but neither of them knew who would be left out.

I tried to tell Debby that it wouldn't be her.

"He's not an old girlfriend," I said. "I don't have to break up with him."

"I wish he was an old girlfriend, then I could be angry and jealous without feeling guilty."

"You feel guilty and you don't even like him—how do you think I feel?"

"I know it's hard for you," she said, "but I can't think about him all the time the way you do. I've got to decide what to do about me. When I graduate, if I don't have a job or a place to go, they'll get on me to come home. You know what that will do to me."

She told me about a week later, nonchalantly, when I looked up from my reading. We were in her apartment. She had already brushed her teeth, I heard her puttering around in the kitchen. I was working on my dissertation, a study of a seventeenth-century book on melancholy. She waited until I looked up.

"Thinking," she said, "or can I talk?"

"Talk," I said.

There was Clearasil on a tiny spot at the base of her nose. She wore an oversize Michigan T-shirt that fit her like a short nightgown. She didn't come to the table where I sat but pulled herself up to a window ledge across the room.

"I told Barbara that I'd go to Chicago," she said.

"I'll drive you to the airport," I said. "When are you going?"

"Not for a visit. To live. After graduation."

"Where does that leave me?"

"Wherever you want it to."

"What's that supposed to mean?"

She hopped off the ledge and came close. "Come with me," she said.

"Just like that, come with you?"

"Why not," she said.

"And where will I work?"

"I'll support you. You'll study melancholy and I'll make you happy."

"You know I can't," I said.

"I know you could."

"Lay off," I said. "I can't decide anything yet."

"Maybe you can't," she said, "but I have to. I need to make my own plans."

"And I'm not in them?"

"Don't be stupid."

"That's what it sounds like."

"It doesn't have to sound like anything. I'm only telling you what I have to do. You decide what you have to do."

I closed my book, packed up my papers.

"What do you expect?" she said.

"I expect you to talk to me, to tell me things, to decide together, not just tell me you're moving to Chicago. Aren't we a couple?"

"Sometimes we are, but most of the time it seems like you and Rocky are the real couple."

I slammed the door as I left.

The next day I didn't go home for dinner with Rocky and I didn't call Debby or go to her house. I stayed in the library until midnight and then went home to sleep.

Rocky was speaking to me only on official matters. He no longer came in to shake my shoulder at seven; instead he let the teakettle whistle until he heard me open the door. He didn't put out a plate for me—but he left the oatmeal on the stove and the rolls in the bread box. For lunch I was on my own.

I was fed up with both of them, but more angry at Debby. I knew how to handle Rocky; I had spent my life living around and with his ways. I knew how to do it. I could get him to accept things, but it was tricky. In high school when I started playing poker on Saturday nights he called me a gambler and threatened to expose me to the school principal, so I figured out a way to co-opt him. I began putting 10 percent of my winnings, usually a dollar or a dollar and a half, into his cap when I came home. Even when I lost I put something in.

"You always win?" he asked.

"Most of the time. I'm a good player, I don't take any risks. If I don't have the cards, I fold."

"So it's not like you're gambling."

"It's more like investing. The most I can lose if I'm careful is two or three dollars. We only bet nickels and dimes—a quarter on the last card. If I concentrate, it's like a job."

I'd said the magic word. He kept his 10 percent, and when I gradua-ted from high school he unwrapped his handkerchief of my poker money and bought me an Elgin watch. That's how it went. Most of the time he was against everything I did until I made him see it in a new way. But it wasn't all one-sided; he made me accountable, too. In poker, because of the way I described it to him, I never bluffed. I did treat it like a job.

He wasn't just in the apartment, he was in the air around me, an angry opinionated fairy godmother/grandfather, who gave me not only my wishes but his, too. From him I expected opposition, and coping with it had formed me. He could get away with most anything—Debby couldn't.

The next day, when she called me, I blamed her for overreacting to the spitting incident.

"A few minutes before, he'd been turned down for that handyman job—for three weeks he'd been frustrated trying to find a room he could afford. Then he saw me playing instead of working and he got a little wild. . . ."

"You'd make an excuse for the guy," she said, "if he had killed every kid on the playground."

"Don't be absurd."

"I'm not absurd. You told me that your mother can't handle him, your sisters can't . . . he doesn't have any friends. . . ."

"He did—they're all dead."

"I don't want to hear excuses, rationalizations. I don't care who he is or what he does—I just want him to leave you alone—to leave us alone."

"You don't just walk away from your family."

"My mother is family. Wouldn't you agree that it's smart to get away from her?"

"That's different. She's got money and influence—real power in the world. Rocky's got nothing. He had his work, now he's got the synagogue three mornings a week and he's got me."

"Well, he doesn't have me," she said, "and he's not going to."

When she hung up she called Chicago and told Barbara she'd arrive the day after graduation.

Nineteen seventy, my last spring in Ann Arbor, happened without me. Usually when the weather turned I couldn't stand to stay cooped up in the dry air of the library. Life was outside in the diagonal. In the classrooms people couldn't concentrate; by the dozens classes moved

outside—English, history, psychology—all on the new spring grass. Occasionally I noticed an economics class outdoors—complete with blackboard and a professor in a suit and tie drawing diagrams. After five months
of dreary gray Michigan weather, when the sun came out and stayed, it
was almost as if the gray stucco buildings melted away, leaving only the
grass and healthy young bodies in T-shirts and shorts. That spring I stayed
in the library. During the first two weeks of glorious sunshine I wrote two
chapters of my dissertation. I didn't see the sun and I didn't see Debby.

When Rocky received a letter inviting him for an interview, I drove
him to the Detroit Jewish Home for the Aged. He wore his brown suit
and dark red tie again, and he seemed no more grim than he had been
for the last few weeks. I took it as a good sign when he told me twice
that I was going the wrong way on I-94.

I tried not to think about the home. I put it out of my mind just as
I tried to put Debby out of my mind. That effort was great for one thing:
I concentrated on "Melancholy" and did six months' work in those two
weeks.

Rocky had kept his duffel bag packed to show me that he meant
business. If he really went to the home, I would have what I wanted—
but if it happened that way, I wasn't sure I would still want it.

The home we looked over that afternoon in late April was a solid
red-brick building with a well-kept lawn and trimmed hedges.

The rooms were doubles—utilitarian, but they had carpeting, desks,
lamps, closets, and bathrooms—vastly better than the Vaughn Street
room he had chosen for himself.

Rocky knew that it was merely an interview, but he insisted on
taking his duffel bag along. "What if they get an opening right away
while I'm there?" he said. "It's full of old-timers—they can die from a
bad fart."

"Then they go to the waiting list—they don't just let in whoever
happens to be in the office."

"That's what you think," he said. "If there's a room and they see
you can take care of yourself and probably won't eat too much—you slip
them a ten spot or a twenty and they let you in."

I didn't tell him that slipping someone a ten might not even get you
a good seat at a Tigers game anymore. Rocky lived outside the flux of
money mostly because my mother and I protected him by paying for

almost everything; but it went beyond that. He never let the country get too big—he kept everything on a local scale the way he had in his Lithuanian village.

America might be two hundred million people and a trillion-dollar economy, but what did that matter? Rocky never had a bank account. He paid his bills by walking to Wurzberg's Department Store, Consumers Power, the gas company, or the telephone company. He counted out dollars and change to the penny. Every six months he paid twenty-five dollars on the three-thousand-dollar life insurance policy that he'd bought in 1919 and paid for in its early years at twenty-five cents a week.

In the supermarket he paid attention only to the prices of what he bought—flour, sugar, butter, yeast, eggs. They weren't expensive. He saved a little of his $120 Social Security check every month.

Though he offered to pay half, my mother covered the rent. We didn't tell him it was $220 a month or he would have moved out. It was expensive by graduate student standards, but well worth it, I thought, for the quiet neighborhood where Rocky took his long walks.

We furnished the apartment with odds and ends from our home in Grand Rapids. Nothing matched. The red-and-white-flowered chair stood out against the green carpet, and the sixteen-inch TV looked as if it would crush the thin-legged wooden table that supported it. The single wall decoration was the big gilt-edged mirror, the one my sisters had used to practice their debate gestures.

The only new thing was a dinette table, a mistake because it had no Formica top. We kept it covered with a thick plastic tablecloth, and at his spot, Rocky sometimes added a piece of oilcloth to catch spills.

I shopped without Rocky when I bought the chicken, the meat, and whatever else was expensive. Rocky's Friday night favorite, fishheads, was free; nobody else in Ann Arbor seemed to want them. Between us we didn't have much money. I realized how little as I filled out the forms for the home. I was earning $420 a month as a teaching fellow at the university. That plus his $120 put us a little above the poverty level that had only recently been formulated by the Johnson administration.

I was exhausted from carrying his duffel bag all the way from the parking lot. As a sign of spring or maybe even his mood—he wore the two-tone shoes. In the lobby I put the bag down to rest while he walked into an office to announce his arrival. I felt foolish standing there with about seventy pounds of clothing and the Babylonian Talmud. I had warned him not to try slipping anyone a ten spot, but I was certain he'd do it.

A half dozen residents sat on the leather couches. A man approached slowly from the men's wing. When he came to a spot about ten feet from the couch, I knew who he was. He grabbed his trousers just above the knee as if he wanted to keep them from getting wet in a puddle. Holding his pant legs, he waddled to the couch. I knew the habit. At our house he used to grab his pants as soon as he walked in. I think he did it to keep the creases straight. In his youth it might have been a sign of chivalry—my friends and I had nicknamed him Highpockets. I hadn't seen him since I graduated from high school—had no idea he was still alive.

He had just let go of his trousers when I reached out my hand. He was bent but still a big man. His soft cool hand dwarfed mine.

"Mr. Schneiderman," I said, "do you remember me?"

When I told him my name—he did. Rocky, standing near the administrative office, called out for me to get the duffel bag and come in.

"Rocky," Schneiderman said, "you old son of a bitch—you're still alive?"

Rocky stared at him. "I forgot," he said, "that they let you in here." Schneiderman walked over to greet his old acquaintance. It took him a while to get his big body into motion.

"I'm in a hurry," Rocky said. "There's a woman in there waiting to talk to me."

"They got time," Schneiderman said. "They never do anything at this place."

Rocky waited, let Schneiderman shake his hand. When Highpockets tried to embrace him, he stepped back. "I gotta go," he said. "Be well, Schneiderman."

"Don't run," Schneiderman said. "When you get outter there I've got a surprise for you."

"How old is he?" I asked Rocky as I followed him down the corridor.

"Who knows?" Rocky said. Carrying the duffel bag made it hard to keep up with him.

I recognized the name of the director of admitting from her letter.

Mrs. Okrent, a pleasant woman in her early fifties, laughed when she saw me with the bag.

"I'm sorry," she said, "didn't the secretary tell you this was only a preliminary interview?"

"The secretary told me," I said, "but try telling him."

"If it makes you feel any better," she said, "you're not the only one who has brought luggage to an interview."

"You see," Rocky said, vindicated.

As she walked us through the building Rocky was not only polite, he was courtly. He motioned for Mrs. Okrent to lead the way, he opened doors, he praised "the good paint job" in the rooms and hallways. He picked up a sheet to see who made the mattress and told the director that the home had Simmons mattresses, the top brand.

"I didn't know that," she said. "Thank you."

When we returned to her office, Schneiderman was there, along with a man in the kind of gray felt hat that 1930s gangsters wear in the movies.

"Excuse me," Mrs. Okrent said, "we're in the midst of an interview."

"Harry Zeff," the man in the hat said, presenting himself as if he were a business card. He was about five five and wore a silky gray suit that must have fit him once when he was fifty pounds heavier.

"Harry Zeff," Rocky repeated. I couldn't tell if he was pleased or not. I remembered the name, but not the person.

"And this must be the little kid," Zeff said, looking me over. "What a little momma's boy you were. I had a Henry J. convertible, remember that?"

I did.

"And you were a little *momzer* maybe five, six years old, and you kept bothering me for a ride."

I remembered.

"But the mother, the grandma, Rocky, they wouldn't let go of you even to ride around the block. They said you'd catch a cold in the convertible. You still a momma's boy?"

"We didn't let him go," Rocky said "because we didn't want him in the car with you, and we were right. You're a regular gigolo."

Mr. Zeff had dated one of Rocky's cousins, a bosomy widow named Bashel. Now and then they took a Sunday drive all the way to Grand

Rapids to see us. About Bashel and Zeff I recalled only the names, but the Henry J., I could still see its chrome-tipped fins.

"She was way too old for me," Harry Zeff said.

"And way too good," Rocky added.

Mrs. Okrent tried to make peace. "Please, Mr. Zeff," she said, "would you mind waiting outside? We'll be done in a few minutes and then you can chat as long as you'd like."

"I don't wanna talk to him," Rocky said. Then he turned to Zeff. "Are you still selling dead men's clothes?"

"What does he know?" Zeff said, addressing the rest of us. "I had a war surplus store, he thought I robbed graves. You spent too many years with your head in an oven, Rocky, you got nothing upstairs and you never did."

"I know a crook when I see one," Rocky said, "and you're the world's biggest gonif."

"A gonif!" Zeff said, raising himself to his full height. "Tell him, Schneiderman. You've seen it."

"He had his picture in the paper," Schneiderman said.

"I'm not a gonif," Zeff said, "I caught one. I did the cops a favor. She knows, it's in the file."

We all looked at Mrs. Okrent. "Mr. Zeff," she said, "had some notoriety."

"I was on channel two, channel thirteen, they all wanted me."

"The Angel of Death should want you so bad," Rocky said.

Zeff, filled with his own glory, ignored Rocky and launched into the tale he was destined to tell forever.

"It was in the hat store, my last business on Roosevelt Avenue, Harry's Hats. This *schwartzer* comes in, says he wants a hat with a feather.

"I say, 'You want a straw, a bowler, a felt, a fedora, a Stetson, whatever. You pick a hat, I'll stick in a feather free of charge.' Could I have treated him nicer? The *schwartzer* pulls out a gun and sticks it against my heart and says 'Gimme your money.'"

In Mrs. Okrent's tiny office, barely big enough to hold all of us, Zeff acted it out. He was the crook who wanted a feather, Schneiderman played the role of Zeff.

"You think I was scared?" Zeff asked. "Not me. 'I wipe my ass with guys like you,' I told him. 'Get out.'

" 'I'll get it myself,' he says, and while he's reaching with his fat hand to punch No Sale, I grab the switchblade I keep under the counter and I cut off his nose."

"His nose?" I asked.

"You shoulda seen it," Zeff said. He demonstrated on Schneiderman but stopped short of the other man's face.

"Did he live?" I asked.

"He lived. They even sewed the nose back on, but he'll never rob another hat store. There won't be any more hat stores," Zeff continued, "mine was the last. I closed it and moved in here."

"Why'd you let him in?" Rocky asked Mrs. Okrent.

"Gentlemen," Mrs. Okrent said, "enough." She walked out of her office. Rocky hurried after her. I grabbed the duffel bag and followed.

Zeff stuck his head out of the office door. "I hope you come here, Rocky, and live a long time. That's the worst I can wish for you. Live a long time, but not on the same floor as me."

Mrs. Okrent walked us to the car. She was trying not to laugh too much. "Everyone here knows the story," she said.

"Throw him out," Rocky said, "or I'm not moving in."

"We can't do that, there are policies, procedures. You know that. Anyway, it's a big place. You wouldn't have to see too much of him."

She said we'd hear from the admitting committee in about a month.

When we got back to Ann Arbor I dropped Rocky at home and went to campus. In my mailbox there was a note from the rehabilitation ward of the hospital. "Mr. Kerner," the note said, "will be able to leave the hospital for a brief outing Saturday night. Will you be able to take him?" It was the last day of April. He had been shot in early September. He hadn't been outside the hospital grounds for eight months.

Chapter 11

*U*nable to reach me that day, Kerner had the nurse try Debby's apartment. I didn't tell him that Debby and I hadn't been speaking to one another. He was too persistent and questioning. If I told him anything, he never let me get away with a short answer. Anyway, during our two-hour reading periods, whatever talk we could sneak in was barely enough time to discuss his problems. In that setting, I had no complaints worth uttering.

Kerner felt otherwise. Catastrophe had not reduced him to generalities. He wanted all the specifics, the trivia, of the life that he was, for the time being, missing.

Debby called me. "Are you gonna take him out somewhere?" she asked.

"Of course," I said.

"Can I come, too?"

"Sure."

"Are you still mad at me?"

"Yes," I said.

"I'll try to stay out of your way, then—I just want to be there—it's so exciting after all these months."

Debby had only met Kerner once, when I wheeled him down to the cafeteria. The two of them spoke for a few minutes, awkwardly. Even before he was shot Kerner made people uncomfortable. He would ask you something like what mattered most to you in the world after he'd known you for five minutes. When he asked Debby she pointed to me.

Where to take Kerner and how to do it occupied me, but I thought about it even more because I could hardly wait to see Debby again. Kerner had asked our mutual friend Alan Perlis to come along, too. Perlis, the star of our department, was a handsome, muscular New Englander. He had given up his time off on a Ford Foundation grant that year to teach Kerner's freshmen classes. He worked without pay so that the university could give the meager salary to Kerner.

In addition to being Kerner's close friend and mine, his strength would help us with the big wheelchair. Kerner needed extra support for his back and neck—a high-backed chair that was hard to fold and to fit into the trunk of a car.

When Alan and I asked Kerner where he wanted to go, he told us to surprise him. We didn't want to surprise ourselves. We borrowed a wheelchair from the hospital and practiced taking it apart. It wouldn't fit into the trunk of Alan's Volkswagen beetle, but in my Chevy we could squeeze it in. We decided to take him to a movie and went two days ahead of time to the State Theatre to request special parking and to look over the building and the layout and see if there would be stairs to overcome and where the restrooms were and what access we would have. In 1969 there were no curb cuts in the streets—no laws required special parking for the handicapped. Alan and I wanted this first outing to be as flawless as possible.

I didn't consult Debby, I was still playing my angry role. She called me on Friday. "I got tickets," she said, "to a concert for all four of us."

I had thought of it, too—every spring Eugene Ormandy and the Philadelphia Orchestra came to Ann Arbor for the month. There were a few student tickets, but it was mostly for older music lovers and the wealthy patrons of Detroit.

Kerner loved music. Every day he spent hours in the ward with his headphones on, blotting out the humdrum of rehabilitation. While people worked at exercising his limbs, he would close his eyes to enter Mozart's world. I envied the way he could so quickly be transported.

"Third row center," Debby said.

"It must have cost a fortune."

"It did, but that's what credit cards are for."

"Forget it," I said. "I don't want your mother paying for this."

"It's all right."

"Fine," I said, "until she sees the bill—then she'll make you pay in other ways. It's not worth it, we'll go to the movies. I already figured out a route and have special parking."

"Hold on," she said, "you're not listening to me. My mother offered to pay—she suggested it."

"I'm amazed," I said.

"You shouldn't be—she does have a heart."

"I still don't like it," I said.

"Whether or not you like it isn't the point, is it?"

"Okay," I said, "Mom treats. Is this a date for us?"

"Do you want it to be?"

"I don't know," I said. "There will be Kerner and Alan; you're not crazy about it when there are other people involved."

"Other people don't bother me, with one exception. But do we have to fight about that again? Let's just take Joel out; that's enough for one night."

Alan and I scouted out Hill Auditorium. It was a lot more accessible than the State Theatre. There was a ramp and special parking.

Helen, the enforcer, was on duty when we came to the ward at six-thirty to pick him up. She made us wait until exactly seven. Debby and Alan had never seen her before.

"She acts like it's a prison, not a hospital," Alan said.

I had heard her lecture to Joel about the importance of schedules, especially for the handicapped. "If you let the clock get away, you let your life get away," Helen said. I think she had a point. I saw how some of the people in the ward dozed through their days. Not Kerner. If he wasn't studying or listening to music or dictating a letter, he was plotting his return to Israel.

"Have him back at ten," Helen said. I pleaded for an extra half hour in case there were multiple encores.

"We can't just slip out unnoticed," Kerner reminded her.

"Ten-thirty," she said, "no later."

When we got to Hill Auditorium all our plans fell apart. In the traffic we couldn't get anywhere near our special parking place. When we did, it was occupied. Then, when I finally parked, far from the auditorium, we couldn't open the trunk. A strap from the chair had jammed the lock.

The crowds walked past on their way to the concert. Kerner sat on the front seat and watched the passersby. Alan and I struggled with the trunk.

Finally at eight, a half hour after the concert began, Debby took out the backseat and crawled into the trunk.

Kerner pleaded with us to stop. "Don't waste the tickets," he said. "The three of you go. Nothing's gonna happen to me."

Debby, slithering into the trunk, managed to open the tool kit. Using a screwdriver, she pried open the lock. When the trunk popped open we cheered as if it were a football game. Alan pulled out the chair, Debby followed. Her face was sweaty and streaked. Trunk dirt decorated her light yellow dress.

By the time we got to Hill Auditorium it was after nine and the intermission was already over. The ushers wouldn't let us in. Debby was furious—she wanted us to muscle our way in.

"I don't care if the whole orchestra has to stop," she said. "We're going in." Alan was threatening to write an exposé for the *Michigan Daily*. Kerner ignored us all. Seated on his chair on the broad porch of the building, he looked up at the Doric columns and beyond at the spring sky. When Debby and I arrived, ready to use his chair as a ramrod to force our way in, Kerner stopped us.

"Just leave me here," he said. "I haven't seen the sky for eight months."

We sat on the steps next to him and waited. He wasn't looking for particular stars or for formations. He was glad to be where he was— outdoors and alive.

"I don't need a concert," he said. "This is a concert."

We believed him, but we still felt as if we had failed, and after all our planning.

"Where else do you want to go?" Debby said. "This time I promise the trunk will open."

"If it's not too much trouble," Kerner said, "I'd love to go see Rocky."

It was already nine-thirty, an hour past Rocky's bedtime. Before I could say so, Debby started pushing the chair toward the car. "Sure," she said, "no problem."

I caught up with her and shook my head. I didn't want to explain to Kerner. She ignored me. "Anyone," she said, "would rather see Rocky than the Philadelphia Orchestra."

"I would," Kerner said. "I really would." She got a running head start trying to push the chair up Hill Street but still needed Alan's help for the steep grade.

I got her alone when Alan took over. "Why are you going along with this?"

"I'm not going along. Once you get in the car I'll go home. Rocky won't kick him out, will he?"

When Debby didn't join us, Kerner began to figure things out. By the time we reached my apartment, he was actively meddling.

"I'll talk to him," Kerner said. "Rocky listens to me."

"Please," I said, "he's okay now. Let's not get him started again. Just let him enjoy seeing you."

Alan and Kerner waited in the hall while I woke Rocky. He came running out in his long underwear to embrace Joel. Once in the apartment he started to pull Kerner out of the wheelchair into the red-and-white easy chair near the window where Rocky liked to sit while he read the paper. It hadn't occurred to Alan or to me that our friend was not glued to his wheelchair. He enjoyed the easy chair and the cinnamon rolls that Rocky heated for him after he got dressed. Rocky even put on a tie in honor, he said, of such an important guest.

He pulled out a prayer book and helped Kerner recite the prayer of a person who has lived through a life-threatening experience. "Blessed art Thou, Lord our God, King of the Universe," Kerner read in slow Hebrew. Rocky corrected every mistake.

"Louder," he said. Kerner continued. "Who bestows favors on the undeserving, and has shown me every kindness."

Rocky said, "Amen." Alan and I had tears in our eyes. When I could, I reminded Joel about his curfew.

"Forget it," he said, so I did.

"Now that I can get out of the hospital," Kerner said, "I'm going to start coming to the synagogue. I'll see you there."

"We need you," Rocky said. "All the students sleep late. Be there by seven o'clock, earlier on Mondays and Thursdays."

"He can't get out of the hospital at seven in the morning," I said.

Kerner laughed. "I'll tell them Rocky said I have to be there on time."

"It's not a joke," Rocky said.

"I'd like to practice a little Hebrew reading," Kerner said. "Would you guys excuse us for a while?"

Alan and I took a walk, telling one another how wonderful it was to see Kerner so much himself in spite of everything he had lost.

When we came back to the apartment Rocky was holding a cup of hot coffee to Kerner's lips. He'd already spilled a lot on Joel's shirt and the wheelchair, but it didn't seem to bother either of them. On his own Rocky had transferred Joel back to the wheelchair. They were having a good time.

We stayed at the apartment until almost midnight. When Alan and I wheeled him into the ward, Helen was in her cubicle of an office, talking on the phone. She walked quickly to us.

"Leave," she told Alan and me. We were already helping Kerner into his bed.

"You're almost two hours late," she said. "I've had hospital security looking for you."

"Did you think I'd been shot again?" Kerner asked.

"You're not funny, and you have no respect for authority," she said.

"You're right," Kerner said.

She glared at me. "You're responsible. I am revoking your special privileges. You can't come here to read to him anymore—not that you've been studying. I know you've just been visiting him."

"What's so terrible about visiting?" Alan asked. He was more surprised than I was. He hadn't seen Helen before. I thought she would be off duty by eleven, so I didn't worry much about being late, but she was working a double shift that Saturday night.

"If they hadn't put you in bed," Helen said, "I would have made you sit in your chair all night—to teach you a lesson."

"If you ever do that," Alan said, "I'll break *your* fucking neck."

She ordered us both out again. We were walking away and were already at the far end of the ward when we heard her scream. She had bent to straighten Kerner's pillow. When he had a good angle, he locked his teeth onto the starched white shoulder of her uniform.

Her scream woke some patients, and the ones who woke up cheered for him. Helen called the resident on duty to give Kerner a sedative. In the morning a psychologist and a social worker came to visit. All three told him that a graduate student should know better than to bite.

For a week I was banned from visiting. The social worker made it the goal of his therapy to have Kerner apologize. The hospital officials called a family conference. His father and brother flew in from the East Coast.

Joel treated it all as a comic episode. He had something bigger in mind. "I knew that night," he said, "that I was ready to leave. I talked it over with Rocky."

The Helen episode gave the hospital a reason to speed up his exit. When his father and brother visited, he told them his plan: he was going to Israel, and so was his ninety-five-year-old buddy.

Chapter 12

*I*n May I received a graduation announcement from Debby. Since we still weren't talking to one another, she didn't know that I would be there anyway. Writing furiously, at least partly because I wasn't seeing her, I finished my dissertation before the deadline. I too would graduate in June.

I called to thank her for the announcement.

"Are you gonna be mad at me forever?" she asked.

"I'm not mad," I said. "You made your decision about Chicago. That told me everything."

"You're really pretty stupid," she said. "If this was happening in a book, you'd know what the guy's supposed to do."

"I'd read the last page to find out."

"Then you'd miss all the fun. You're missing it now, and so am I. Will you meet me for coffee?"

We sat in one of the dark wooden booths at Drake's again, and George watched us through the window.

"Why are you so stubborn?" Debby said. "You're not even giving me a chance."

"You made up your mind."

"So what? Make me change it. What do you want me to do?"

"I want you to marry me," I said, "you know that."

She moved over to sit next to me. "Okay," she said, "I will."

We were kissing in the booth when George snuck in as someone opened the door. Jealous, he jumped between us. The manager made us leave.

We walked the streets of Ann Arbor, too happy to talk about it. As if he were announcing it, George ran ahead, barking. I walked Debby to the playground, where she was still working. We told the kids. They started calling her Mrs. Rotten Apple.

We decided not to discuss the problems. "We'll deal with all that later," she said. "Let's just be happy now."

I went back to my old schedule of spending most of my time with Debby. Rocky didn't seem to mind my absence. He had his own little secret.

He and Kerner had made their deal that night in our apartment. Kerner asked him to keep it quiet until everything was arranged and he had the tickets in hand. Rocky had been keeping the duffel bag packed for Israel as well as for the home.

He announced it to me casually. "Right after Pesach I'm going to Jerusalem." I thought he was speaking metaphorically, announcing his death.

"Are you sick?" I asked.

"I'm not sick, I'm going to help Kerner." I didn't believe him, but that night at the hospital Kerner confirmed the statement.

"I need an attendant," he said. "The insurance company will pay for someone, why not Rocky?"

"He's not strong enough to push your chair and to pick you up."

"Actually he is," Kerner said, "but my brother's coming, too. Rocky wouldn't let me buy him a ticket until I told him I needed him. He'll only come if he can call it a job."

I called my mother. Together we worried. We knew that Rocky would try to do all the physical labor—a danger to him and even more to Kerner should Rocky drop him or lose his grip on the wheelchair in the Jerusalem hills.

"He can't go," Bashy said, "unless you go along to keep him under control."

I wanted Rocky to see Israel, but not as much as I wanted to marry Debby. "I can't do it," I said. I told her half the reason. "I've got to finish my dissertation."

When I explained all my reservations to Kerner, he understood, and he had a quick answer.

"Can Bashy go, too?" he asked.

On her trips to Ann Arbor, my mother always visited Joel in the hospital. When she was young she had wanted to be a nurse. She was very good at helping him. Kerner, motherless since he was six, let her be as maternal as she wanted.

"She'd have to make arrangements for someone to take care of the business, but she probably can."

"Good," he said, "then they'll both come with me."

"It's too expensive," I said, "to take them both."

"Not too much at all," he said. "It's cheaper than hiring people and setting up an apartment here. Look, I'm going to Israel anyway. If I have the two of them and my brother, I'm going with a family."

When I still hesitated, Kerner settled it. "Think of it as a wedding present," he said.

Rocky tried to pretend he wasn't excited, but he had been packed since the day Kerner told him.

On the day of the flight, Bashy came to Ann Arbor, and I drove the three of them to the airport. Joel's brother would meet them in Jerusalem.

I helped Kerner onto the plane. Bashy sat next to him, Rocky at the window seat behind, his running shoes not quite touching the floor. He could hardly wait for the takeoff. When the stewardess asked him to strap in he said he wasn't afraid—he was going to Israel. I strapped him in and kissed each of them good-bye.

"Thanks for the wedding present," I told Joel, who was no less excited than Rocky. "I hope he doesn't drive you nuts."

"According to the hospital staff," Kerner said, "I'm already nuts."

In June, while I marched up to receive my degree and shake hands with the president of the university, Rocky was in an apartment on Jabotinsky Street in Jerusalem. Kerner and Bashy sent me cards. Rocky, they said, didn't find any synagogue that satisfied him, but there were so many that he complained about a different one each day.

I even got a letter from him. He told me, in Yiddish, that he was coming back because he was too old, but if he was younger, eighty or so, he would stay and work on a kibbutz. He liked all the fruits that grew in Israel—he reminded me that it was indeed a land of milk and honey.

With Rocky in Jerusalem and all the test taking and writing finally behind me, for the first time I had entire days to spend with Debby. We jogged together through the arboretum, we bicycled to the malls, went to three or four movies a week. The only problem was our marriage. Debby told her family.

Her father, a businessman who specialized in avoiding family life, had his usual no comment.

"If my mother told him that an earthquake had destroyed China," Debby said, "and that it was a good thing, he wouldn't disagree with her. He'll do anything to keep from stirring things up at home."

Harriet first took our announcement as a sort of April Fools' joke. When Debby persisted, she switched tactics—treated her daughter like an eight-year-old playing dress-up.

"You're not getting married and that's final," she said. "This isn't some ridiculous peace march you can decide you want to be in on."

"Mother," Debby said as I listened to the telephone conversation, "I am getting married. I'm not asking for your permission."

"And you're not getting it, or one penny, either."

"Good," Debby said. She knew the money threat was coming. That was Harriet's usual opener.

"How will you support yourselves?"

"He'll sell drugs, I'll work the streets, and when the children come they'll beg."

"It's all a game to you, isn't it?" Harriet said. "You'll learn that life is not a game."

"I've heard this one."

"Obviously not enough."

"Too much," Debby said. "Look, we're getting married. I'm sorry you're not happy about it."

"You're twenty years old," Harriet said. "You'll meet other men."

"You mean richer men."

"Yes," Harriet said, "and better looking and smarter and everything."

"Thanks, Mom," I said from the extension phone. She paid no
attention.

"If you don't do better, you can always marry him. He'll wait. He's
got enough books to keep him busy."

"If that's all you've got to say, I'm hanging up."

"Wait a minute," Harriet said. "Is he still on the line?"

"I am."

"Forget all of this," she said to me, "and I'll put a check in the mail
tomorrow. Ten thousand dollars—all yours."

"You're even worse than I thought," Debby said. She hung up.

"Well?" Harriet asked me.

I hung up, too.

The next Sunday her father invited me out for lunch. He had to be
in Detroit for business, so he would journey thirty-five miles out of his
way to meet me. He didn't invite his daughter; it was going to be the
two of us, man to man.

"He'll offer the money again," Debby said. "Maybe he'll up it—I'd
guess he'll go to twenty."

"I'm holding out for fifty," I said.

"Don't joke about it. It's not funny to me."

"You know I don't mean it."

"In their world, everything's for sale. If you say that to him, he'll
believe you."

"I said it to you, not to him. I'm sorry."

Other than Rocky, money was the only thing that got to her immediately. "It's all they've got," she said, "and the last thing I want."

When Ben, her father, extended his limp hand to me, I half expected that he'd have thousand-dollar bills up his sleeve. As it happened
he didn't mention money or Debby or the marriage. He was a quiet, darkly
handsome man. Uncomfortable with words, he would have preferred to
have his wife take care of our meeting. I could tell that this was his
assignment. She had nagged him to take me to lunch.

He started by talking golf as if I were a stranger who had a particular
course in common with him and not a particular daughter.

"I don't play golf," I finally told him.

He understood that this meant we needed a new subject. I read a mild panic in his eyes. He didn't have another subject—at least not for me. He was no fool; far from it. In his steel business, Debby told me, he had made millions. But when he wasn't talking about plate or sheet or reinforcing bars, he seemed to draw a blank. I let him lead the conversation, and only once, at the end of the meal, did he even come close to our subject.

"Women," he said, "can cause a lot of trouble."

"Are you referring to your wife," I answered, "or to Debby?"

"Women in general," he said, then he started telling me about the high-quality rebar that came from Mexican minimills. He called for the check. I thanked him, and we shook hands.

I had come ready to engage him. Instead I felt as if I'd spent an hour in a lukewarm wading pool.

"Our family is divided in an exact way," Debby told me when I tried to explain the emptiness of that lunch. "She's in charge of everything, and he supplies the money. Now you understand how he's lived with her all these years."

"Does this mean he approves of me?"

"It means," she said, "that he'll do anything to avoid getting into it with her. I'm sure he likes you. He's a sweet man, and he likes things to stay on an even keel. He's happy when he's at the shop."

Harriet telephoned twice a week and never asked about the wedding. It seemed as if she thought my lunch with Ben had been all I really wanted. I thought about calling him to ask if I'd missed something or if maybe he'd misunderstood me and thought I'd said something about changing our plans. Debby advised me to ignore her parents. We planned our own wedding, on July Fourth at the playground. I liked the idea of being married at home plate. She was in the process of getting permission from the school district to use the field. I wrote to my mother and Rocky in Israel, realizing how lucky I was not to be telling him in person.

A few days after my proposal we had decided what we'd do about Rocky. At first nothing. He would stay in the apartment, I would move to Debby's. I wouldn't come back at three A.M.—but I would come over every day for at least one meal. If he spoke to Debby and acted decently, he could come to her apartment, too, whenever he wanted.

"Don't count on it," I said.

Technically he was still waiting to hear from the Detroit Jewish Home, but I knew that especially after his run-in with Zeff, he'd never go. I was in the process of applying for a teaching job. If I got one, we'd have to move; then it would be his choice. If he wanted to come along, he would live not with us, but close by. Debby and I each gave in a little. With Rocky in Jerusalem, planning his future and ours seemed a lot easier.

When Debby finally gave up the idea that there was a chance to have me without him, she was philosophical.

"No place is perfect. There are earthquakes in California—tornadoes in the Midwest. . . . I'll just try to think of him as a natural disaster."

"I'm sure he'll do the same for you."

"Too bad," she said, "that we can't buy insurance against one another."

Chapter 13

Rocky returned from the Holy Land on July 1. When he came through customs, he handed me a plastic garbage bag of dirt almost as heavy as his suitcase.

"For my grave," he said. "Put it in."

I knew what he was referring to. All pious Jews want to be buried in Israel, but a symbolic bit of earth from the land of Israel is the best that most can do.

"A teaspoonful would have been enough," I said. "You brought back ten pounds. Did they ask you about it at customs?"

"Everybody brings it back," he said. "They didn't even look. I could have brought more."

We left him to watch the luggage while Bashy and I went to get the car. I finally had a chance to ask her how he'd responded to the news of my wedding.

"I didn't tell him," she said. "What would I have done if he got mad and said he wasn't coming back with me? I was going to tell him on the plane, but I didn't want him to make a fuss there, either—anyway,

I thought, in a few hours he'll be home and you can tell him. You can handle him better than anyone."

"This time I was hoping I wouldn't have to."

"You shouldn't have to," she said. "Thank God you didn't let him get in your way. I don't know what he's got against Debby."

A few hours later I found out. I gave him time to sleep off his jet lag, put his Holy Land dirt in his underwear and socks drawer, and have his coffee and herring lunch. Then I told him.

He picked up the newspaper, went to his chair, and began to read. I waited a few minutes, then I started to worry that he wasn't feeling well, that something had happened to him in Israel.

Thinking about the dirt did make me a little melancholy. When a ninety-five-year-old talks about furnishing his grave, you take it seriously. Finally he spoke. "I'm glad you're getting married," he said. "I want you to get married. I always wanted you to get married. I got married, your father got married—that's the way it should be. Only not her."

"Okay," I said. "Why not her?"

"She's no good."

"What's no good about her?"

"She stuck out her tongue at me."

"You threw her out of the house."

"I had a right to throw her out. She moved in like a gypsy in the middle of the night."

"She didn't move in—I invited her. Don't forget that."

When he picked up his newspaper, I went to the kitchen to think of a better approach. The last thing I wanted to do was go over and over the trivial complaints he had about Debby. That annoyed me and fueled his anger. What we were talking about had nothing to do with Debby. I wanted to let him know that I understood how this must feel to him.

I stayed in the kitchen, as if the twenty feet that separated us as he sat on his easy chair would give me the distance I needed to talk about what neither of us had ever put into words.

"I'm not going to get married and forget about you. Wherever we live there's always going to be a place for you."

He didn't look up from his paper. "Don't worry about me, I can live wherever I want."

I let him have his bravado. "Sure you can," I said, "but what about me? What am I gonna do if we live far apart?"

"You'll call on the telephone."

"You never talk to me on the phone."

"You'll write letters."

"I could write every day and call, too, but you know that's not enough. I wanna see you every day."

"Then marry somebody else and I'll come over."

"You keep coming back to silliness—it's got nothing to do with Debby."

"You want her," he said, "forget about me." He tossed his paper onto the coffee table and stormed outdoors.

When I told Debby, she said that Harriet had told her almost the same thing when she agreed to give us a wedding.

"All right," she said, "if you're going to go through with it, I'd rather have you get married in our house than on a playground, but why does it have to be him?"

Harriet's objections were pretty straightforward. She wanted a son-in-law she could be proud of, someone rich or likely to be—a doctor, a lawyer, a businessman. Instead, Debby chose "a bookworm who lives with his grandpa," and even worse, a local bookworm. Because I was from Grand Rapids, some of her guests would know me. She wanted her daughter to do better, that made sense. Rocky wouldn't admit to anything that rational. He stuck to the tongue complaint. I felt foolish, but I finally confronted Debby with the charge. She didn't laugh.

"What will satisfy him, cutting off my tongue?"

"He's just grabbing at straws," I said. "He doesn't have an objection, but he's taken his stand and he won't back down."

We tried to make peace. First an apology. Debby agreed to try.

"Dear Rocky," she wrote, "I'm sorry if you think I stuck my tongue out at you." I made her leave out "if you think."

"So I have to admit to sticking out my tongue."

"Yes," I said. She crossed it off. "Proof that I love you," she said. It didn't matter. Rocky threw away the note.

"What more do you want?" I screamed. "She apologized, now you can be a mensch, too. I've got a hundred things to do before the wedding. Stop torturing me about her tongue."

"Do whatever you want," he said. "Forget about me."

"I will," I said, and for the next three days I tried to.

Harriet hadn't spoken to me, but I understood that more than a month earlier when she agreed to the wedding she was compromising as much as she could. Debby and I decided to match her gesture. We let her plan the ceremony just as she wanted it, allowed her to limit our guests, pick the flowers and Debby's dress. Her heart wasn't in it, but she put up a good front.

I did my best to please her. One of my undergraduate friends, Stanley, already a lawyer in Washington and an excellent dresser, selected a gray Brooks Brothers suit for me. I had my curly electric hair cut bridegroom short and tried to look as much like a doctor or a lawyer as I could.

On the day before the ceremony Rocky and I drove to Grand Rapids. We spent the night before my wedding in our old bedroom. It was going to be a small family wedding in Harriet's living room, but on the wedding day morning, faced with glorious sunshine, Harriet decided to set up the chairs in the yard. Bashy left the house early to play with Bailey's two sons. Bailey and her family were staying with one of Bailey's friends. At noon, my sister Maxine sent her own family ahead and waited at the house to drive Rocky. We decided it would be best to let him stay home until the last minute so he wouldn't add to what was already a tense atmosphere.

I tried to read in the morning but couldn't concentrate. I retied my tie a half dozen times. I didn't want to get to Harriet's house too early, either. At one o'clock Maxine ran up to my room. She was crying.

"He's not going," she said. "I had him almost to the car and then he ran into the basement—he locked himself in. What shall we do?"

I tried to stay calm. "Leave him to me," I said.

"You shouldn't have to do this," she said, "not on your wedding day. I can't believe he's doing this to you. You know how much he loves you."

"That's exactly why he's doing it. Leave the little gonif to me," I said. Just using that Yiddish idiom to describe him made me feel confident. An hour before my wedding he was making me play my oldest role—I would have to placate him, bring him not downstairs, but this time upstairs into the warm and now widening world of his family.

Maxine was still crying when she got into her rented car.

"I'll be there in a few minutes," I said.

"Don't let him ruin this for you."

"I won't," I said. "I can handle him."

It was a few minutes after one as I stood outside the basement door. Ours was a deep unfinished Michigan basement, cold even in July. He had snapped the security latch from within so there was no way for me to enter. To see into the basement, I would have to get down on my knees to look through the tiny window that hadn't been cleaned in years.

There were only appliances in the basement, an empty freezer, a washer, a dryer, and a mangle, the automatic ironer that had once seemed so modern to us and now rusted slowly from the bottom up.

If I was going to be on time to my wedding, I had about twenty minutes to lure him out of that dark place. I started out gruff, businesslike.

"C'mon," I said, "we haven't got much time. I'm waiting for you."

He didn't answer. I yelled. "Do you hear me?"

"I hear you," he said. "I'm not going."

I put a piece of newspaper down on the bare dirt near the window so I wouldn't stain my trousers. Through the clouded glass I saw him sitting on a wooden chair, one long ago discarded to the basement. Above him glared an unshielded hundred-watt bulb. He looked like a prisoner in solitary confinement. He hadn't put on his brown suit; he wore everyday clothes, a short-sleeved blue shirt, patterned blue trousers, and the Adidas Dragons I had given him. The clothes told me he meant to stay put. He liked to dress for occasions—today he had dressed for the basement.

I broke down when I realized that.

"Look at you," I said, "sitting there like a prisoner in a cage instead of coming to my wedding. Is this what you want?"

"Yes," he said.

He showed no emotion, didn't look up to see me peering into the window.

"No matter who I'm marrying, if there's anybody in the world who should be there, it's you—don't do this to yourself."

He didn't answer. I didn't have any more time. "You'll be sorry for the rest of your life," I said, "and you're not going to stop me."

"Go ahead," he said, "do whatever you want."

When I left the window, I sat in the car for a minute or two, then I even drove about fifty feet thinking he might come out of the basement. I knew that if I could get my hands on him, the contact of the flesh would do what words couldn't. He would not have resisted the tears streaming down my cheeks as I sat behind the wheel. He knew that as well as I did, and he stayed in the basement, keeping his feelings and himself hidden.

At a quarter to two I drove to my wedding. In the pictures I'm smiling as I sign the marriage document, shake hands with the rabbi, hug Billy, my college roommate and best man, and pose with Bashy and my sisters. In the pictures you can't see what's missing.

I didn't see Debby that day until she walked down the little cloth aisle spread over the grass of her backyard. She asked me with her eyes where he was. We had no rehearsals, but he was supposed to stand beside me. The rabbi chanted. Debby looked, in her white gown and tiara, so beautiful and bridelike that I was glad we were in a more conventional setting than home plate on the school playground.

I was marrying the woman I loved, and not even Rocky could stop me, but he could and did keep me from enjoying it. When Debby asked me again with her glance where he was, I stuck out my tongue.

Chapter 14

I felt more angry than married. During the ceremony I didn't pay attention, all I thought about was that stubborn old man in the basement. At the reception, as Harriet and Ben's friends shook my hand and occasionally slipped an envelope into my pocket, I kept checking the door to see if maybe he had come late by cab.

We went to Stratford, Ontario, for our honeymoon. It was the least expensive place that still felt like going away. It was only a three-hour drive, but you had to cross the border.

We had been married two days and were canoeing on an artificial lake near an imitation of Shakespeare's Globe Theatre. The lake was full of mosquitoes. People who looked as if they were enjoying themselves kept rowing past us.

Debby knew what was wrong. "Maybe he would have come to the ceremony," she said, "if you had invited him along for the honeymoon, too. That's probably what he was holding out for."

"I'm sorry," I said. "I just can't stop thinking about him. I never thought he'd do this."

"Seems in character to me," she said.

"You're probably right. I'll try to be better company."

We rowed for a few more minutes.

"Is this a honeymoon?" Debby asked, "or a school trip?"

"I vote for school trip."

"Me too," she said.

"Shall we call it that and have a honeymoon some other time?"

"Great idea," she said. We packed and drove home. In the car I could hardly wait to give him a piece of my mind.

"I've gotta settle things with him before I can relax and feel officially married."

"Wanna do the whole thing again so he can stand us up a second time?"

"No, I just want to let him know how I feel."

"Don't you think he knows?"

"I want him to understand that he let me down, that I felt abandoned."

"Why don't you just lay off? That's what you always tell me. Nothing's going to change him."

"I'm too pissed. If I don't have it out with him now, I don't know what I'll do. I may start being mean to you."

"Do me a favor, don't confuse us. I'm your new roommate, the one who spits less."

At the border the customs inspector took our car apart looking for drugs. He even checked the air filter and felt around the insulation under the hood. We had to take out the backseat and pull up the carpets. We left before noon and didn't get home until six. It didn't help my mood. I took a quick shower and was ready to go see him.

"What are you gonna do?" I asked Debby.

"I'll go pick up George. Maybe after you give him hell we can go to a movie or something. Even if it's only a school trip, we can still liven it up a little."

He was watching the news when I walked in. "That son of a beetch Nixon," he said, "started the bombing again."

About our little war he didn't say a word. He offered me a cinnamon roll and coffee. He acted as if his only problems were in Cambodia and the Mekong Delta. I shut the TV and was ready to tear into him, but he disarmed me. On the kitchen table in front of him, next to his soft-boiled egg, was the old book of great speeches. He had it open to the Gettysburg Address.

"You still remember it?" he asked.

My father now and then came across books in scrap piles. If they were fairly clean, he brought them home. We didn't buy books—there was a public library for borrowing. The ones my father found became our private library. *Reader's Digest Condensed Books* dominated, along with stray volumes of various encyclopedias, home improvement manuals—we kept anything that had a solid binding. When my father brought in a volume of *Great American Speeches*, Rocky and I read the Gettysburg Address.

He didn't know all the words, and I didn't know what Gettysburg was, but if Abraham Lincoln spoke it, that was enough for us. He read it to me in his Lithuanian accent, which is how I imagined Lincoln delivering it.

Lincoln was Rocky's only postbiblical hero. In kindergarten I knew the address by heart. Every few years he'd ask me to recite it, partly to make sure I hadn't forgotten, but also, I think, to give him the pleasure of hearing Mr. Lincoln's words spoken by me.

"I remember it," I said.

"Say it, then."

"No."

"What will it hurt you to say it? I'll tell you the words if you forget some." He picked up the book.

"Why should I recite the Gettysburg Address? You didn't even come to my wedding."

"What's that got to do with the Gettysburg Address?"

"Everything," I said, "everything's got to do with it. You undermined everything you've done for me by hiding in the basement. I'm not gonna forgive you."

"I'm not asking you to," he said.

"You're worse than a Republican," I shouted. "I don't trust you anymore."

He slammed the book of speeches shut and went to the bedroom.

"You don't have to lock yourself in again, it's over. You lost."

"Get out," he said.

"Why should I?" I asked. "It's my apartment."

"Then I'm going."

He walked outside. I didn't follow him, but I was still raging, getting ready to attack him again when he came back.

When the news ended and it got dark, I went out to look for him. The grocery store at the top of our small hill looked closed, but I walked up—sometimes he sat on one of the benches near the free scale. I didn't find him.

In the other direction, farther downhill, Milford Road turned briefly woodsy, a few hundred yards of yet undeveloped apartment land. I had seen surveyors, so I knew there would be building soon. I hoped he wasn't there. I stepped a few yards in among the trees and called to him.

"C'mon out, I've got more to say."

I was sorry I said it that way. I was already more worried than angry. It was eight o'clock, his bedtime. I walked the length of the area, calling his name. I started to fantasize that he'd decided to sleep outside because I had reminded him that it was my apartment. I looked under trees for him.

I came out running and checked the apartment. He wasn't there. I went back to the woods to look again. There was nowhere else he could have gone. It was too long a walk to the bus stop, and the buses didn't operate after six.

"Rocky," I yelled, "I'm sorry, come in the house."

I was mad at him for this, too, but far more worried. By nine I was frantic. I decided to drive through the main streets of the campus in case he had walked or hitchhiked there. Then I would check the synagogue.

In the car I found him, asleep on the passenger seat.

"Four score and seven years ago," I yelled, "our fathers brought forth on this continent a new nation . . ."

"Louder," he said.

I went on to the end.

"Good," he said. "The Gettysburg Address is always beautiful."

We walked back to the apartment together. Even though it was late he seemed alert after his nap and rewarmed the cinnamon roll for me. We were both calm.

"I'm going to the home," he said, "this time for sure." He turned on the TV.

"Will you have a TV in your room at the home?" I asked. "Otherwise you can take this one."

"What'll you use?"

"My wife has one," I said.

It was the first time I had called Debby that. I said it with extra emphasis, trying to make my point without yelling at him.

"All right," he said, "as long as you don't have to waste money on a new one."

A call from Debby interrupted us. Rocky listened to my end of the conversation.

"Someone stole the dog?" he asked.

"Can you believe that? Nancy, the girl Debby left him with, says he's half hers. They used to own him together—then she moved to the dormitory last year. She never even came to see him. They wouldn't let her keep the dog in the dormitory overnight, so she gave him to this woman, and now the woman and her kids won't let him go."

"What are you gonna do?"

"Debby called from a pay phone. She's gonna sit on the woman's porch. She's not leaving without him."

"Good," Rocky said.

"I'm going there," I said.

He didn't even ask—he just followed me out the door. He got into the backseat.

"Get in the front," I said.

"No," he said, "that's for your wife."

When we arrived at the house where George was held captive, Debby stood and ran to the car. The front shades were down in the two-story frame dwelling and the porch light was on.

Debby stopped when she saw Rocky on the backseat. She gave me a mean look. "It's confusing enough," she said. "Let's not make it worse. I just wanna get George and get out of here."

"Nobody can give away what's not theirs—that's what the communists do," Rocky said.

Debby nodded—she didn't know whether he'd blow up if she spoke to him.

"Let me try," I said. I walked onto the porch and rang the bell. No one answered. I rang a second time, then a third.

"Get out of here," a woman's voice yelled, "or I'll call the cops."

"I'm not leaving without our dog."

"I mean it," she said, "I'm calling the cops. All of you sitting on my porch, you're scaring the kids. They wanna go to bed."

"I'm sorry," I said. "Give us the dog and we'll go."

"Listen, I'm dialing right now and I'll press charges."

"So will I," Debby said. She had joined me on the porch, and Rocky stood at the curb, near the parked car. Debby, more bold now that I was there, walked to the side of the house to look into the windows. She found a shade that wasn't down.

"George," she yelled. She knocked on the window. "Over here . . . woof."

I ran to the window. A boy about eight held George on a leash. The dog barked wildly. A large woman in her mid-thirties put a finger to her ear so she could continue talking on the phone. She saw the two of us and hurried to pull the window shade. We still peeked in since the shade didn't reach to the bottom. We could see George's feet. The boy was trying to pull him upstairs.

The woman ran to the front door, unbolted it, and yelled, "The cops are on the way." She thought there were only the two of us—she didn't know Rocky was on the porch. "Who are you?" she said.

"Never mind who I am; the dog is theirs." George broke away from the boy, and the woman turned to help her son catch him. Only a light screen door kept us from George.

Rocky pulled it, kicked it, then pulled again. The flimsy eye hook pulled through the molding. The screen door came off in Rocky's hands.

"George!" Debby yelled. "C'mon, boy."

Trailing the leash, he came flying off the porch steps.

The woman screamed when she saw Rocky holding her screen. She slammed and bolted the inner door.

By the time the Ann Arbor policeman arrived, Rocky had put the door on its side and examined the damage.

"Cheap labor," he said. "She probably put it in herself."

The woman opened the door a crack for the policeman. Her three children huddled near her. I almost felt sorry for them.

"All I want to know," the cop said, "is, who does the dog belong to?"

He had taken the leash and pulled George over toward the police car.

As if he were King Solomon himself, the officer directed the woman to stand at her door. He sent Debby across the street to stand near my car. He let go of the leash.

"Okay," he said, "both of you call him."

George, a black mutt of no particular distinction, perked up his ears. Debby called for him in a plaintive wail. The mother, joined by her children, drowned her out. George, stopping first to raise his leg against a tree, ran straight to Rocky.

Rocky reached into his pocket. "Here's a ten spot," he said to the officer, "so she can fix her door and have enough left to buy her kids a dog."

He took out another bill. "And for you—go buy yourself a beer after work."

Rocky led the dog to my car. The cop, too surprised to respond immediately, took a minute before he gave Rocky back his dollar. By then George was in the back and so was Rocky.

"Thanks, Rocky," Debby said. She extended her hand. He shook it.

"Come over," he said. "I'll give the dog something. Who knows whether they even fed him."

George had a pack of hot dogs, Debby and I ate herring. She closed her eyes and swallowed a few bites. After that, I felt really married.

Chapter 15

When I received a job offer in Houston, I asked Rocky what he wanted to do.

"I'm staying in Ann Arbor," he said.

"Bashy's moving to Houston with us."

"Who needs her?" he said. "I'm staying here. I'll get a room."

"We've been through this," I reminded him.

"You just go ahead—don't worry about me."

After my failure to convince him to come to the wedding, I lost some of my confidence, but this time it seemed to me that he was making a rather tame last stand—he was willing to talk.

"I know you want to stay here," I said, "but I have to leave—it's my career."

"Who's telling you not to—you should go there."

"What's the difference," I said, "if you live in Ann Arbor or Houston? You'll have a shul there, too, and Houston's a lot warmer."

"I've been in Michigan . . ." He stopped to count. His lips moved silently. "Sixty-five years . . . how am I gonna move, at my age?"

"You already moved at your age when you came here."

"That was different. I could come by bus."

"So you'll move, but only to places you can go by bus?"

He nodded.

"Then it's settled, you can take the bus to Texas."

"You take the bus. I'm staying here."

"What's Michigan—is it Vilna? Is it Jerusalem? It's just a place."

"If I go," he said, "I'm taking all the furniture."

Ever so subtly, he had changed the terms. He wouldn't go without a fight, I knew that, but the fight was going to be about furniture. I had him.

Bashy, ready for a new start, wanted to give the heavy couches and the dining room table and china closet to the Salvation Army. She thought of Texas as a gigantic patio furnished in rattan, chrome, and glass. I took up my old job as mediator. The couches stayed in Michigan, the dining room set came to Texas.

He and Bashy moved to a one-story tract house two blocks from where Debby and I bought a house. Rocky moved out on the first day because of the air-conditioning. He showed up at our front door ready to join us if Debby and I would turn off our air-conditioning. The temperature was in the nineties and the humidity just as high. I understood that the chill affected him, but I couldn't make life unbearable for the rest of us. At his house, I crawled into the attic and shut off the vent to his room. At our house there was a glassed-in porch that had no air-conditioning, so he had a hot room in two houses, yet he took up his primary residence at a location he chose himself. He sat under a chinaberry tree in front of his house for most of the day.

He moved a table and a lawn chair outside. For about five months every year the chinaberry tree served as his study. He came in for quick meals and for his nap. The rest of the time he read the oversize, fixed-by-Scotch-tape Babylonian Talmud in the suburbs of Houston.

For most of the day George sat at his feet, waiting to attack motorcycles if they dared to roar past. People who drove by grew accustomed to seeing the old man and the dog outside. Rocky's skin tanned evenly, emphasizing his bright blue eyes even more. He looked like a yeshiva cowboy.

He said he would never stay indoors for long, but two things made him change his mind. First, we had a baby. If there were any bad feelings left over from our premarital days, Jessica's birth drove them away for both Rocky and Debby. Watching Rocky and Jessica, I realized how it must have been for me when I was a baby. Rocky became Jessica's living playground—his ears, his hair, his animated face, his polished shoes, his tie, his gruff whisper—he lay on the floor and let her climb and explore.

The second event that brought him indoors for a while was the Watergate hearings. He watched all day at his house and then came to our house for the repeats on public television. In front of the TV Jessica copied him, clapping her hands when Nixon had a bad day. I was sure "son of a beetch" would be her first words.

I turned the thermostat way up. Jessica sat with him for hours, sucking along with her formula the sweetness of Rocky's revenge.

Poor Nixon. I was no admirer, but among his many failures he wasn't to blame for Rocky losing his house on Lane Avenue. Rocky was no mere observer of the hearings, not when he knew a participant. He dictated to me a letter to Gerald Ford, urging our former congressman not to accept Nixon's offer of the vice presidency.

Dear Gerry,
I knew your father. He bought rye bread and doughnuts from me and I bought paint from him, flat paint and enamel. Both were good, and he gave me a discount even though I never asked for it.

It's bad enough that you're a Republican, but you shouldn't tie up with that sonofabeetch Nixon. You should go work in the paint factory instead of that.

I heard that your father died a couple of years ago. I'm sorry, but what can you do. I hope you didn't sell the business.

Rocky from the American Bakery

His grudge against Nixon went back to 1923. He had worked for nine years, saved enough money to bring his wife and two children to America, and a month after their arrival creditors took away his house and furniture. He moved his family to a few rooms above the bakery and began all over again, but he carried the memory of that injustice, and fifty-one years later Nixon was paying for it.

I tried to set the record straight.

"Nixon had nothing to do with your house on Lane Avenue."

"People like him did it," Rocky said, "the ones that take advantage of the workers."

"Nixon should be tried and convicted only for what he did, not for what people like him did. There are millions like him—do you want to put them all in jail?"

"Yes," he said.

Jessica clapped. Her hero could say no wrong. She couldn't talk yet, but Rocky stood her on a stool, gave her a small rolling pin, some flour, and dough, and let her work alongside him.

There were fewer breads and rolls that summer. Debby noticed.

"Is Rocky feeling okay?" she asked. He usually baked so much that we had to give the overflow to our neighbors.

"He only bakes while the congressmen go to lunch; he doesn't want to miss a minute of the hearings."

Debby was not as happy during that year as Rocky. We had decided to have children quickly so she could later have a career uninterrupted by childbirth.

"Then," she said, "when they're teenagers maybe we'll have a few more."

It sounded easy, but motherhood plus moving to a new city confined her. The transition from hippie to housewife was too much to do in a flash. We were used to dropping in on friends unannounced, going to movies at the last minute, eating whatever was in the refrigerator. With my university job came a whole series of rituals—dinner invitations a month in advance, departmental gatherings, teas. "My mother would like this," Debby said. "I keep thinking these people are her friends—not ours." She was restless and found it hard to make small talk with my middle-aged colleagues.

"I know they mean well," she said, "but when they start talking I feel like I'm back in class and should be taking notes."

When we had made the rounds, when almost everyone in the department had invited us, we knew we had to reciprocate.

"I can't do it," Debby said. "It's just crazy for me to act like a dinner party is the way we do things. Can't we have a picnic instead?"

I thought a picnic would be fine and nothing even better. "People don't expect you to invite them back," I said.

"They do," Rocky said, "and you have to." He had a European sense of manners. He offered to bake for a hundred or more.

To counter some of the routine of child care, Debby had enrolled in a filmmaking class at the university. The use of an eight-millimeter camera came with the class. She decided to hit two birds with one stone.

"We'll have a party," she said, "and I'll film it, then we'll have another party and show it a few months later. That will count as two and should get us off the hook for years."

"It'll be too boring to film a party. And how will you do it? You can't be the hostess and the director at the same time."

"You'll see," she said.

She got the idea from Rocky. He couldn't stand our sloppy housekeeping; neither could Bashy, but she tried to mind her own business. Rocky wouldn't think of it. At the store he bought plastic bowls, first for Jessica's leftover baby foods that we kept in the jar, then for all our leftovers. Looking into the refrigerator, Debby got her inspiration.

She mailed invitations. My colleagues looked at me a little puzzled. She had invited the polite staid professors and their wives to a Tupperware party.

"The games will be great to film," she said, "and if we sell anything, we get free prizes." The prizes were what sold Rocky.

At the party the saleslady whipped out a curved plastic tool designed to start the orange-peeling process. Rocky won it in a game of passing the orange under the chin to your neighbor. He gave it to me.

The party was a flop. Only four guests came. Debby and I walked the block, inviting neighbors to join us. Rocky held the microphone, Debby the camera. The Tupperware lady, a far better host than we were, greeted the guests.

In the film, when the saleslady described the Tupperware Pyramid of Progress, Debby put in a Gertrude Stein poem as the sound track. As the Tupperware dollars mounted, Gertrude Stein asked over and over, "Is money money or isn't money money?"

We didn't try again. Debby finished her film at other people's Tupperware parties.

While she filmed and Rocky and Jessica watched Watergate, my career began. I sold a story and received five hundred dollars. Rocky couldn't believe it. I had to show him the check.

"Someone paid you five hundred dollars for a made-up story?"

"That's right," I said.

He considered it an act of divine mercy.

Debby and I agreed on how to spend the money—actually it was her idea. She had been watching Rocky while I was mowing the lawn.

"He's like George watching you eat, he almost salivates when the motor starts."

She was right. Lawn mowing was the one big job Rocky still craved, but I couldn't give it to him. I didn't fight him about garbage. He'd pull his to the curb and then walk over to do ours. He baked, of course, he polished shoes more than any of us needed or wanted, he watered the lawn, he baby-sat, but he wanted a hard job. His body still ached to ache. I understood that, but lawn mowing in the Houston heat wore me out. The most I could do was let him sneak in a few minutes whenever I went inside for water. I'd leave the motor running on purpose, he'd grab the handle and begin to push almost at a run. He made the most of the one- or two-minute bursts I gave him. I'd come out pretending to be angry, he would sulk for a minute and then begin to point out the spots I had missed or done badly.

"With the money, let's get him a riding mower," Debby said. She was in the seventh month of our second pregnancy. I remember her sitting atop one of the mowers at Sears, holding Jessica in her lap and pretending that she was going to start the engine and mow right over the sporting goods and backyard barbecues in the next aisle.

"Shall we get this for Rocky?" Debby asked. Jessica grabbed the wheel. She wasn't two yet. I had visions of Rocky letting her drive, and I had second thoughts.

He had never driven a car, and he had no patience. Maybe a riding mower was too dangerous. It was a red Murray with a wide seat and slots for the driver's feet. The steering wheel lay flat, like a semi's, and there were controls for the brake and blade height. The blade itself lay under the machine.

"If he's sitting up there," Debby pointed out, "he's in the safest position of all. There's no way he can get near the blade. It's a lot safer than what he does now, watching you and running over to point out every spot you miss. I always worry that something's going to shoot out from underneath and hit him."

She convinced me. I borrowed a pickup truck and unloaded the mower around the corner. Debby and Jessica made sure he wasn't looking. It took me a while to start it, but when I came rolling along the sidewalk with the blade raised, Rocky burst out laughing.

"It's for you," I said. I handed him the key to the starter. He wasn't nearly as excited as Debby and I were. He got on and steered it around the lawn. Then he shook his head.

"You use this," he said. "I'd rather push."

Chapter 16

*F*or one brief period Rocky, Debby, and I were all working in separate but connected ways. Debby started it by opening a store. Ever since we'd been in Texas she'd wanted to work, but like so many women in that era just before the women's movement blossomed, she felt guilty about leaving Jessica, even with baby-sitters like my mother and Rocky.

We were bicycling home from the ice-cream shop one day when we stopped to have a look at an old house that was being remodeled. We met the owner, a wiry, nervous man named David. He said the house was going to be a craftsman's mall. He had one space left, the glassed-in ten-by-fifteen upstairs porch. We looked up at the room, almost hidden in branches and gleaming in the late afternoon sun. We couldn't resist. For $100 a month we rented a treehouse.

Debby turned it into a tiny health food store. She also stocked wooden toys made by a few local people who let us sell their goods on consignment. David operated a restaurant downstairs, and the three former upstairs bedrooms now housed Bobs—Bob the potter, Bob the jewelry maker, and Bob the leather worker. In the hallway Janice sold belt buckles and leather hairpieces. On our porch Debby installed the toys alongside herbal teas, spices, scented soaps, peas, beans, and lentils.

Jessica was her assistant. My mother and Rocky donated the crockery jars that Gootie had carried from Lithuania and had used to make mead, a kind of honeyed beer. Debby filled them with lima beans and Texas reds. Rocky also donated himself as a worker, though retailing was not his strength.

It was rare enough that a restaurant customer ventured upstairs, still more rare that they went beyond peeking in the door of our shop. If someone actually stepped in, Rocky growled, "What do you want?" If the customer didn't answer specifically and right away, he wanted nothing to do with her.

He didn't like the types who wandered in for a look. "Why don't they stay home and eat? You see by their dresses and the big cars they drive that they've got plenty of food at home."

When I tried to give him lessons in salesmanship, Debby agreed with Rocky.

"They are assholes," she said. "They think it's so 'cute' that I work in this tiny place. A couple of them have asked, 'How do you make a living, my dear?' "

"He's still gotta be polite," I said.

"Why?" Debby said. "The ones that just wander around and sniff at things don't buy anyway. If he gets rid of them, I can read."

From the restaurant, David, who had no experience in the food business, constantly called on Debby to help. He had a long lunch menu and a cook who regularly didn't show up. He would come up, wring his hands, and beg Debby to close the shop and help in the kitchen.

"You don't have customers anyway," he said.

Debby liked that kind of bluntness. She would go into the kitchen; sometimes one of the Bobs would, too. Holding Jessica, she would look for the ingredients they needed to fill an order. If it wasn't in the kitchen, David would apologize to the customers, wring his hands, and urge them to walk through the shops. Then he'd run across the street to the supermarket to buy what he needed.

After four years of being a housewife and mother, Debby was back in the kind of chaotic atmosphere she liked. We never quite made the $100 a month for the rent.

"Do you care?" Debby asked me. "I hate to lose the money."

"It's an investment," I said, and it was. She had an eye for absurd detail. Almost daily she came home with good stories. I let them expand in my imagination. I sold one about a fervent vegetarian. This time Rocky decided that I had discovered something. He moved into high gear.

"If they'll pay him five hundred dollars again for a story," he told Debby, "they'll pay me five thousand dollars." He went to work.

"How many pages do I have to write?" he wanted to know.

"You've got to write until you come to the end of the story."

"What I write won't be a story," he said. "It's all true, and so many things happen that it could go on for years."

"Good," I said. "Let it go on, the longer the better."

I was happy that it kept him occupied. He wouldn't tell me what he was writing, he just announced page quantity every few days.

"Twenty," he said. "Is that enough?"

"I can't answer unless you let me read it."

"Do you let me read yours?"

"Do you want to?"

"No," he said. "I don't like made up. I like true."

"I like true, too."

"You wouldn't understand this."

"Who will?"

"People who know more than you."

Of all the things he did, nothing amazed me more than the way he went at writing. He was almost one hundred and had a total cataract on one eye. He had refused surgery because he still had the other eye, but it too was clouded over. I tried to use his writing as the reason for him to agree to the cataract surgery. "How can you write when you can't even see? I have a friend who's an eye doctor, he says he can do it in a half hour. One night in the hospital and that's it. You'll see fine again, and you'll write ten times as much."

"I see plenty now," he said. "Tell your friend to line up customers someplace else."

He sat at his desk with the same kind of attention he gave to Watergate. Sometimes, when he came out of the room, I saw a look I recognized, the one that keeps every writer going, the one that shows you've pleased yourself.

"It's going okay?" I asked.

"You can take all the money," he said. "Once I'm finished it's yours."

"You think it will bring in a lot of money?"

"Hah," he said, and he went back to work.

Debby, closing in on her ninth month, decided to try meditation. For Jessica we had done the Lamaze method. I went to the classes, timed panting women with a stopwatch, and then in spite of perfect attendance had been banned from the delivery room. I was arguing with an administrator when a nurse came out and put Jessica in my arms.

"All that panting is baloney," Debby said. She wanted to try meditation for its own sake and maybe as some help in childbirth.

We went to the class with one of the Bobs, the leather one. The teacher, a blond Texan with a drawl, lived in a conventional apartment community. You knew he was a meditator because his apartment was decorated with statues of Buddha.

"Ah've lived in an ashram," he said, "and ah've known masters who have taken the light."

We sat in a circle and had to keep our eyes closed all the time. He taught us some yogic breaths, some ways to concentrate on color, but mostly we sat in silence, or we said "om" together while we breathed deeply and listened to the universe. Just when he was winning our confidence with a series of firebreath exercises, the instructor would open his eyes and say something like "You know, they're having a sale at Ming Galleries, twenty-five percent off on all the Buddhas."

One of the exercises in the six-week meditation class involved sending a psychic message.

"Like this," the instructor said. He closed his eyes. "I'm concentrating on my sister, who lives very far away up north in Canada. She's had a lot of trouble. I haven't spoken to her in months. In fact, she doesn't want to talk to me—but I get through to her like this. 'Hi, Mary Ellen— you take care of yourself now.' I did that aloud so you could hear—now everyone close your eyes and send a message to someone you want to contact. Concentrate hard."

"I can't believe we're paying to do this," I whispered to Debby.

"Sh," she whispered. "That's my spiritual message—don't steal it."

I sent a message to *Esquire* magazine, where I had sent one of my stories. I didn't think I'd get an answer, so I sent one to Rocky next. I told him to have his cataract fixed. We all held hands while we "sent," then we hummed. At the end of the session the instructor put probes on our heads to see if we had approached the relaxation level of alpha waves. I hadn't—Debby was as relaxed as possible.

"You almost put the machine to sleep," he told Debby. "That baby in there is in the deep blue waters of peace."

"Who'd you contact?" I asked Debby.

"You," she said.

"Why me?"

"I was testing the system."

We laughed about wasting our money this way, but a week later the fiction editor of *Esquire* called. I told him I'd been expecting him.

Rocky came around, too. He just decided one afternoon when he couldn't read his own writing that he'd have the cataract out. "Call your friend," he said.

"When do you want to do it?"

"Tomorrow," he said, "in the morning."

I should have known that he'd want it immediately. I'd been with him many times in stores. Whenever he bought a pair of trousers and wanted them hemmed, the clerk would look at the calendar, Rocky the clock. Usually he'd say "Fifteen minutes," sometimes he gave them a half hour. If the salesperson couldn't get the tailor to do it on the spot, Rocky wouldn't buy.

I did call my friend, and I did ask him for the next day.

"First, I'm booked for the week, second I wouldn't touch a hundred-year-old guy. Take him to the medical center."

I made an appointment there for the following month. Rocky grumbled, but I reminded him that he had waited himself, so he couldn't complain.

With one eye he continued to write, and just before his cataract surgery, he handed me the manuscript—ninety-five pages in Yiddish.

"You didn't tell me it was in Yiddish."

"What did you expect, Lithuanian?"

"I can barely read it."

"It's not for you—send it to the magazines. They'll know how."

It had taken him about two months. He had written on unlined white paper—his rows were quite straight and the Hebrew characters all legible. I could tell that he had written it not word by word, but letter by letter.

I shook his hand and hugged him. He moved away.

"Let me congratulate you. It's no small thing to write ninety-five pages."

"When it's in the magazines and they pay you, then you'll congratulate."

He didn't fool me. Even a hundred years doesn't cover an author's pride. He didn't know what fiction was, had never heard of any bestsellers, and in money anything beyond a hundred was a fortune. But he did know from sitting all those hours with his face an inch from the page that one word makes the next one possible and that even when it's all true, the ways in which the truth collects itself into a story can be as tricky as lies.

He drank a cup of coffee and sat down to squint at the television. "It's not as easy as I thought," he said, "but making a good dough is even harder."

I tried to prepare him for disappointment. "You know, most writers don't sell the first thing they write. You might have to work on it some more."

"What do you mean?"

"Change it a little."

"I don't change—it's all true."

"Okay," I said, "then maybe you'll start another one."

"Nah," he said, "that's your job."

He stayed in the hospital three days, because the doctor wanted to be extra careful. Then he wore a bandage for two more weeks. While he recovered I read his manuscript. The hero was a great rabbi of Dubnow, a city in Poland. In the eighteenth century he traveled throughout Poland and Germany, and everyone knew him as the "Magid," the "preacher" of Dubnow. He was such an excellent speaker that wherever he went, the synagogues were filled to capacity. Rocky emphasized the preacher's learning; by the age of eighteen he knew nine tractates of the Talmud by heart.

His piety was also exemplary. He put on tallith and tefillin in the morning and he kept them on all day. On Mondays and Thursdays he fasted. He gave good advice and helped people to observe the law. I missed a lot of words. I read his Yiddish the way a mountain man reads English, my finger on each word. Whenever the Magid traveled, he changed lives. He once found a boy leading a blind man in the street and took both into his own home. The boy grew up to be a great rabbi. On another occasion the Magid met a ne'er-do-well, a taverngoer who had neither a job nor a family. After meeting the Magid, the man changed his ways. Eventually he became the president of a synagogue.

In the moral tales of this preacher I recognized a lot of what Rocky admired, piety and learning and big crowds at the synagogue.

I thought that one day we'd sit down together and translate it into English, but he never asked for it, and soon after he finished I forgot his work. Too many bigger things took over.

Chapter 17

A permanent contact lens solved the problem of Rocky's left eye, then a few months later he had surgery for bowel cancer. He recovered quickly, was home in two weeks and at our house the next day, pulling the garbage to the curb by eight A.M. But I worried.

"He used to have it at the curb by six," I told Debby.

"They don't pick it up until four or five in the afternoon, he's still eight hours ahead."

"He's not the same."

"Maybe he's getting smarter."

"Don't tease me, I can see it. He takes a nap in the morning and one in the afternoon."

"He's one hundred years old and recovering from surgery, what do you expect? He's entitled to slow down." She was right, he was entitled to his two naps and to the longer and longer periods of drowsiness that filled his day. I started to prepare myself for the inevitable.

Debby tried to take photographs of him, though he rarely let her. She got a few beauties, one of Rocky and Jessica baking together. He is wearing her plastic apron with the ABCs. It ends above his waist. Jessica smiles shyly at the camera as if she's doing her best to make up for the angry scowl that her great-grandfather is giving her mother as she photographs the two of them.

There's one of Rocky holding our second child, Sam. Sam, a hundred years younger than his baby-sitter, has his lips on Rocky's cheekbone. With his tiny hands he's going for the cap, as Jessica did, as I remember doing. The children helped him fight the lethargy that was overtaking him.

Sometimes Bashy would call to tell me that he wouldn't eat. I would bring Jessica and Sam. Each pulling him by an arm, they could get him into the kitchen to eat a soft-boiled egg or herring and bread.

He had lived to become the favorite of his great-grandchildren and to see me established in a career. He had overcome cancer and partial blindness and thirty years of forced retirement. He had moved twice in his nineties and made new friends in each place. He still had the energy to go to the synagogue, to study and to fight off air-conditioning. Debby was right; what more could I expect? A four-generation family living so closely together, I knew what a rare thing I had.

In the 1970s I saw myself change from a rebel to a father and a writer, and when the children were both in preschool, Debby started teaching in a community college. The next stage of her life had begun, too. "I want more children," she said, "but I need a while to recover. Give me a decade to think about it."

A decade didn't seem like much when she was twenty-six and twenty-seven and twenty-eight; it was fine for us to think in decades, but not for Rocky.

The clock ticks for everyone, but for Rocky it boomed.

Occasionally he'd mention it. He liked clothes. Over the years I bought him dozens of caps and shirts and trousers, but shoes were harder. He wore a size six, and most men's sizes began at seven. One day I found a size six in a modern version of his ancient favorites, the brown-and-white cordovans. I couldn't resist.

I tore off the price tag, but he knew they were expensive.

"Take 'em back," he said, "I don't need 'em."

I knew he'd say that, so I countered with the truth. "It's so hard to find your size that I would have bought almost any style—but this one, that I know you like, how can I take it back?" I told him what he always told me when I wore new shoes. "Wear these out and then you'll get new ones even nicer than these."

I helped him step into the stiff thick leather. He looked down and liked what he saw. Then he used one shoe to kick off the other before I could bend to help him.

"Take 'em back," he said. "I won't live long enough to get your money's worth."

When I refused to return the shoes he started wearing them daily instead of saving them for Saturday. He was doing his best to get his money's worth. Every time I noticed the shoes I thought of his mortality.

"You know," Debby said, "you're talking yourself into something. He just felt sorry for himself for a few hours, that's all. This guy is not about to leave us. I think he still needs more to keep him busy."

The next morning when he came out to pull our garbage to the curb, Debby was waiting. She told him she had a problem. He came in to drink coffee with her. "I hate to bother you," Debby said, "but I need a little help."

"Whatta you need?"

"You know that I work nights at the community college—Tuesday and Thursday."

"You call that nights?" he said. "You work a couple of hours, nights is all night."

"All right," she said, "let's say I work a couple of evenings, but you know it's all I could get."

"You don't have to tell me about part-time," he said.

"Maybe, if I'm a good worker, they'll give me full-time."

"You don't need that, you've got to stay with the kids."

"In a couple of years they'll be in school, then I can do full-time—full-time is only four hours a day."

He laughed. "You're hard laborers, you and your husband. What do you want me to do?"

"If you can, I'd like you to stick around Tuesdays and Thursdays from, say, one to five. I'll be here, too, but if you're kind of supervising, I'll be able to prepare for my classes. When you need a rest, just tell me."

After his first week of "supervising" we both noticed that he'd perked up.

"He was here a lot of those times anyway," I said.

"But he wasn't working. Now that it's his job he stays awake the whole time."

"It was a great idea," I said.

"There's one big problem," Debby said. "He's driving me crazy. I arrange for a friend to come home from nursery school with Jessica so I can get some work done, but he doesn't like the other kid to be around. Today he told Hilary to go home. You don't tell a four-year-old to go home. She started to cry, and it took half an hour to calm her down."

"Are you gonna fire him?" I asked.

"No," she said, "I'm just gonna change the job."

The next day after Jessica and a girlfriend had lunch, Debby sent them across the street to the park. They went with a security guard. Rocky held their hands crossing the street. Debby carried his aluminum lawn chair and set him up near the playground. Outdoors he was less possessive of Jessica, and the sun made him sleepy.

"We wake him up when it's time to cross the street," Jessica said, "and sometimes when we need a big push on the swings."

Saturdays the synagogue kept him busy, and Sunday when Debby and I jogged together, we did so at the university track so he could supervise the children. Jessica and Sam played in the sand beneath the pole vault, and Rocky sat on one of the judges' seats, watching them. George ran ahead, sniffing the cinders for enemies.

The children liked to meet us at the finish line, holding paper cups of water. Debby saved something for the end. She always beat me by a step or two. "Yeah, Mommy!" the children yelled. She was their hero.

Day by day I knew how fortunate I was to have Rocky so old and still so able. When I ran I sometimes jogged to a silent rhythm, a kind of prayer, not addressed to a namable being, but a wish that came literally from my pounding heart and my quick breath. I prayed for him, for more strength and a painless end.

As it turned out, I should have prayed for another.

Chapter 18

*W*e were at the movies watching a cult film, *Pink Flamingos*, which one of Debby's students had recommended. Most of the audience seemed to love it, but we didn't. I was dozing off when Debby poked me in the ribs.

"How many people do you see on the screen?"

"One," I said.

"You're sure?"

"Of course I'm sure. How many do you see?"

"Two," she said. "It's been like that for about five minutes."

"Probably your contacts," I said. She closed one eye, which solved the problem, but we left because we didn't like the movie.

It started that simply. At first we both joked about the effects a bad movie could have. Debby went to the eye doctor to check her contact lenses. He found nothing wrong but suggested a dentist. He thought that tension in the jaw might be causing her vision problems. The dentist found no tension in the jaw and recommended an ear specialist. Her ears were fine. Debby went to her gynecologist. "Specialists have been all over my face," she said. "They say everything seems okay, but I'm seeing two of you right now." He sent her to a neurologist, who hospitalized her for tests. A brain tumor, he said, could be the cause.

We sat in the X-ray room, waiting for Debby to be called. She wore her own pajamas and a hospital gown over them. We were both terrified.

"It's just this damn double vision," she said, "otherwise I feel okay."

We leafed through magazines together until Debby went for her X rays and CAT scan; then, in the evening, when the neurologist walked in, he told us right away. "It's not a brain tumor."

"Thank God," I said. I kissed the top of her head.

"When can she go home?" I asked.

The neurologist wasn't as happy as we were. He kept her in the hospital to test for syphilis and hepatitis and meningitis, then he checked her spinal fluid to see if she had somehow gotten tuberculosis in the spine. Finally, after they scanned her bones, we had a long conference with the doctor.

"The tests are all negative," the neurologist said, although by the time we received that verdict five days later Debby had become so dizzy that she couldn't stand up without help.

"I'm certain," the neurologist told us, "that it's multiple sclerosis. The only way to diagnose it is to rule out everything else. We've done that."

"What is it?" Debby asked. I didn't know, either, I only recognized the name from the black-and-white public service ads in magazines.

The doctor spent the next half hour telling us about myelin, the white fatty substance covering the central nervous system. When myelin wears away, some nerve impulses can't get through. Multiple sclerosis, he said, is the name of the disease that causes myelin to degenerate.

We asked all the questions we could think of and there were no answers. Nobody knows what causes MS, and there is no treatment. He gave us a thick pamphlet so we could read about it as well. "It could go away and never return," the doctor said. "That happens sometimes. Or it might come back in a year or five years, or it might never go away."

"You mean I might always see double?" Debby asked. She was wearing a black eye patch by then. Not using her left eye seemed to help.

"Right now it's affecting your optic nerve," he said. "It could let up."

"But you don't know if it will?"

"No," he said, "I don't. I wish I could tell you things with greater certainty, but MS follows no absolute pattern. Why don't you read the pamphlet and then we'll talk again." Debby had it open to a page that showed a photo of a man in a wheelchair.

"Will it do this to my legs, too?"

The doctor stood up. "I can't make any predictions," he said. "I can tell you what will happen in a thousand cases," he said, "but not in one."

Unlike that doctor, I can only tell you what happened in one. It has taken a long time for me to forget the medical facts, to put them enough out of mind so that I can recall the Debby who was not defined by a disease.

Debby came out of the hospital determined not to give up anything. She was in the midst of making a slide show for the end-of-year party at Jessica's kindergarten.

She had a plot taken right from life, a dognapping, and two stars, Jessica and George, who got along well. Jessica in her dark blond curls, posing in one of the slides in front of a huge glass candy corn container, was already a heartbreaker. Stuart, her five-year-old costar, looked longingly at either Jessica or the candy. The bad guys, five-year-olds chomping on rubber cigars, chained George in a garage. But in the plot that Debby and the kindergarten teacher, David, wrote, the good children won. George, released from captivity, had dinner at an expensive restaurant.

The five-year-olds loved best of all the slide in which George, seated at a table, scanned the menu. He looked up to make a choice.

Debby couldn't. She held the slide viewer to one eye but couldn't raise her head. "Is it in focus?" she asked me.

Section by section her body deceived her. She lost feeling in part of a toe, in the bottom of her left foot, in the side of her face, in her bladder, in her scalp. There was no pattern. Some of the losses were fleeting, some stayed. When her balance faded she bought a bright red cane. On the bumper of her two-tone Plymouth she put a sticker that said, "Fight the Good Fight." For two and a half years she did.

I had one big job during those years—I looked with her at a tiny screw that held the glass globe of our bedroom ceiling light in place. It was a hundred-watt bulb covered by a two-dollar frosted glass held in place by a five-cent screw. I stared at that screw like a sailor adrift might scan the horizon for some hope of land.

As the dizziness increased Debby spent more of her time in bed. Since everything awful had started with her double vision, I pinned all my hopes on a return to single vision. If she saw one screw, I was convinced there would be one, our life could go back to the unity of the past.

She thought so, too. We were surrounded by friends, by our neighbor Marcy, who was in our house almost as often as the children; by Jane, our carpool friend; by Debby's racquetball partner, Meryl; by Cookie, our PTA friend; by half a dozen great people from the English department who came to read to Debby on a regular schedule. But we were not wholly in tune with any of them. The two of us had our own signs, our own sense of where we stood in the world. We were adrift on our innerspring mattress, looking up at that screw, which had become our North Star, our guide through the darkness. Debby's big toe became our clock. She had a bruise on her right nail from one of her early stumbles. Gradually the discoloration grew toward the top.

"I hope this will be over," Debby said, "by the time the purple grows up and I can cut it."

"Even before," I said. I thought so, so did she. It couldn't be otherwise; she was too young, too healthy, for this strange affliction to overtake her.

Harriet telephoned daily and refused to call the disease by name. She referred to it as a virus, which some researchers thought it was. If calling it a virus instead of MS seemed to make it more understandable, I didn't argue. I couldn't worry about names, I had my hands full trying to keep our life from crumbling.

While Debby lay in bed waiting for the double vision and the dizziness to pass, strangers entered our lives, a string of housekeepers and baby-sitters, one less reliable than the next. Worst of all were the nurse's aides to help Debby bathe and wash her hair.

I started out doing it, but she asked me not to. "I hate to give you this job," she said. "It makes me feel like I'm your patient, not your wife."

"Don't be silly," I said. "I've been giving Rocky a bath for years."

"It's not the same."

She was right. She wanted to hang on to being a wife and mother, not an invalid.

As Debby's disease progressed I spent less time with Rocky. I took the children to his house, where he and Bashy baby-sat, but he didn't come over as often. He didn't know what to do. He was used to going to the store with Debby or helping her with the children, but when she could only lie in bed he stayed away.

No matter how often I tried to explain it to him, he couldn't understand what was happening.

"How can there be something wrong with her brain?" he asked me. "She knows everything."

"It's like a light switch that doesn't work," I said, using one of the analogies I'd read. "You can turn the switch on all day, but if the signal doesn't get through, the light won't go on."

"It must be cancer," he said.

"It's not cancer, I've told you a hundred times."

"Then when is she gonna get better?"

I had no patience for him when he started asking me the medical questions. I had read everything I could about multiple sclerosis, and I had no answers. I understood why the neurologist had been so vague. Rocky didn't. He had lived his century in the world of absolutes. If you were sick, you either recovered or you died. He had no experience with lingering, and I had lost my playful touch with him. Instead of teasing him I just got angry.

"I'm not going to tell you a hundred times," I yelled. "The trouble is in her brain, nobody can tell you when she'll be better."

"And what about you, what's the matter with your brain? You're the one who's acting crazy."

"What do you want me to do," I said, "jump for joy because the Astros won or the temperature didn't hit ninety?"

"You don't have to jump for joy," he said, "just take care of things."

"I'm taking care of everything."

"Take care of your children," he said.

"The children are fine. They go to school, and they have a baby-sitter."

"You don't need the baby-sitter," he said. "Don't throw out the money—I can do it."

Because we always reached a quick dead end when we talked about her illness, both of us took out our anger in the question of baby-sitting.

Sam was three when Debby's sickness began. We could explain to Jessica why she couldn't jump or even sit on Mommy's bed, but Sam wouldn't listen to explanations.

There was Debby right in front of him, propped up on pillows and waiting to tell him a bedtime story. He would escape from the bath towel and get to her bedside before I could get his Batman or Little Slugger pajamas on him.

Rocky was there watching once when Sam ran to Debby, and even while I screamed for him not to do it, he jumped onto her bed and on his knees bounced to her side.

"I want a story," Sam said, "like you used to tell me."

He was burrowing under her arm to hide from me. Debby's face had turned pale. The dizziness was so intense that the weight of a book placed on the bed was almost more than she could bear. I grabbed Sam, screaming, and threw him to the ground.

"Don't you ever jump on Mommy's bed!" I yelled.

He raced past me and tried to reach her again. I pulled him away as quickly as I could. I carried him howling down the hall and threw him into his room. Jessica and Rocky watched.

"You got no business doing that to the baby," Rocky said. "He's not hurting her."

"He is," I yelled. "Don't stick your nose into what you don't understand."

"You're the one who doesn't understand," he said. "Go take him out of the room. Tell him a story."

"He'll stay there until he learns to listen when I tell him something."

"I'm going to get him," Rocky said. He walked toward Sam's room. I blocked the way. "All he wants is a story."

"He'll get it," I said, "when I have time."

"You never have time for anything," Rocky said. "You sit in there like you're afraid someone will steal her. Pay attention to your children." He tried to push me out of his way, but I didn't budge.

Sam screamed and pounded at his bedroom door.

"You're too old to take care of children," I said.

"What I forgot, you and your baby-sitters will never know."

"Get out," I said. "You're making it worse."

"Let the boy come to me first."

I took my hand from the doorknob. Sam ran out. If he had jumped on Debby's bed again, I might have thrown him through the wall. He ran right to Rocky and climbed into his arms. I tried to help Rocky lift him, but they both pushed me away.

"I'll tell you a story," Rocky said as he carried Sam to the living room couch, "about the bakery in Beaver Falls when I first came to America."

He kept Sam on his lap. Jessica sat beside the two of them.

I went back to our room. Debby stared at the bottom of the light. Her face was more pale than I had ever seen it. Silent tears streamed down her cheeks.

I asked my daily question. "How many do you see?"

"Three," she said. "Leave me alone."

Chapter 19

*B*etween 1978 and 1980, Debby's condition deteriorated, and Rocky, who had seemed as if he had one foot in the grave at 102, bounced back into action. He was too busy to die.

We worked out an agreement on the baby-sitting. He didn't do primary care of Jessica and Sam, I kept the baby-sitters, and Bashy helped enormously. But Rocky became what Debby had called him, a supervisor. No detail was too small for him.

He complained because I bought Sam Velcro-snap shoes just when he planned to teach him to double knot; he told me I should be taking Jessica for violin lessons instead of to baseball games. Above all, he started to focus again on the longer range, getting Jessica and Sam through a school year rather than wearing out a pair of shoes.

He went to school with me to find out why Sam's preschool teacher recommended that Sam wait another year before he entered kindergarten.

"What's the matter," Rocky asked her, "you don't think he's smart enough to be in kindergarten?"

I had explained to him that I wanted to keep Sam back a year anyway. His birthday was in November. He could be either a few months young in one class or a few months old in another.

"There's no hurry," I told Mrs. Shaw. "He can do prekindergarten again."

"What did he do wrong?" Rocky wanted to know. "When I cash my Social Security he counts the money perfect and he knows the ABCs and a lot of Hebrew songs."

"He's a smart boy," Mrs. Shaw said, "but he has a lot of trouble cutting."

"What do you mean, cutting?"

"Cutting with a scissors." Mrs. Shaw made a scissors of two fingers on her right hand to demonstrate.

"Cutting?" Rocky repeated.

"Yes." Mrs. Shaw brought her finger scissors closer. Rocky pushed them away.

"What kind of school do you send him to?" he asked me. "Are they teaching him to be a tailor?"

Mrs. Shaw laughed. "He's just a little behind in manual dexterity. Most boys his age are."

"What does he do wrong?" Rocky pressed the issue.

"He doesn't cut straight."

"Who cares," Rocky said, "if he's not gonna be a tailor? Who cares if he cuts straight?"

"Enough," I said. "I want to keep him back anyway."

"The boy counts like a bookkeeper," Rocky said, "and she says he can't cut."

I thanked Mrs. Shaw and pulled Rocky out of her room. It was the end of the school year, and lots of mothers were in the hallway. They were emptying their children's supply buckets, packing up the leftover crayons and wide-lined paper and stickers. I didn't know any of the mothers in Sam's class and hadn't made any play dates for him.

Jessica had lots of friends. After the last day of kindergarten when Debby and David showed the slide play, Jessica spent a summer being invited out. Her popularity continued into first grade, but in second grade she stopped going to the houses of her friends. She just wanted to stay home.

I saw her becoming more isolated, but I didn't do anything about it. She played with Sam. She taught him jacks, and I bought them a little trampoline and baseball gloves and plastic bats and a battery-operated pitcher who lobbed Whiffle balls at them.

Debby had been sick for so long that all of us forgot what it had been like before. The purple bruise grew out, and nothing changed. I stopped asking how many screws were at the bottom of the fixture. Debby struggled to get out of bed. Instead of just reading to her, she asked her friends to help her go to the store. She fell often, but she kept trying. She swam whenever we could find an uncrowded pool. Because she couldn't use her eyes, she began to listen to classical music. At night we talked about the children the way all parents do.

I was settling in for the long run, had given up the innocent hope that things would go back to what they had been. Debby was sometimes depressed, but she was still Debby, until that too began to change.

Within a period of weeks, she lost interest in everything. She stopped pushing herself to get out of bed. Throughout the illness she had always forced herself to get up, especially in the morning to see the children before they went to school. But in the spring of 1980, I had to coax her, give her pep talks to arise even at ten. Sometimes I couldn't do it alone, I had to wait for help from one of her friends. She didn't resist, and usually didn't answer; she just became more and more passive, as if there were no reason to do anything.

When Rocky and I came back from the conference with Mrs. Shaw, I had the last two weeks of Sam's classwork to show her—seven drawings and the obviously uneven cutting.

"Picasso probably couldn't cut straight, either," I said as I held up the preschool artworks. It was past noon and she was still in bed. Her look was so far away that it scared me. It wasn't only passivity, something else was wrong, too.

I put down the drawings. Almost in a whisper I asked her, "Do you know where I've been?"

She hesitated for a minute, then she looked at me. "Alabama," she said.

I showed her the rest of Sam's work, then I called the doctor. When I told the nurse the symptoms she gave me an immediate appointment.

The neurologist examined Debby in his office, then called the hospital to order a room. "I'll have to take some tests," he said, "but it appears that the disease has affected her thinking." He said he wanted to call in a psychiatrist, too.

Debby continued in that dreamlike state. She didn't ask about the children, but on Sunday I brought them. Jessica kissed her, but Sam, fearful that I'd pull him away, stood far from the bed until I carried him over. Rocky and Bashy came in the afternoon and then drove the children home.

Bashy had recognized for weeks that everything had changed. Wisely, she didn't question me. Rocky wanted explanations.

"Why doesn't she talk? What happened?"

"I don't know," I said. "When I know I'll tell you."

I had lost my patience and not only with him. At that time, I divided the world in two, those who could understand what had happened and those who couldn't. I had no time for the nonunderstanders, and I lumped Rocky in that group. He didn't stay there long. When I had a call from someone who introduced herself as a nurse at the Methodist hospital, my heart raced and my mouth went suddenly dry. "We're having a little problem with Mr. Goodstein," the nurse said.

"What happened?" I screamed.

"Don't worry, he's fine," the nurse said. When she heard my panic, her voice became solicitous. "I'm sorry to alarm you, I know a little about your situation from what your grandfather told me. He's angry, but we really can't let him contribute."

"What?" I asked. "What's he doing?"

"He's at the blood bank, he wants to give a pint of blood to your wife. The technician tried to explain that we have regulations. He's listed his age as one hundred and three . . . is he really?"

"He is," I said.

"I thought," she said, "that maybe he was a little confused."

"Is he still there?"

"Yes," she said, "that's why I called you. He refuses to leave."

"I'll come get him. I can be there in a few minutes."

She had called me at my university office, across the street from the medical complex. I jogged to the blood bank and was a little winded when I reached the waiting room. There was a leather couch and four matching chairs and a pitcher of orange juice, but Rocky ignored the comforts. He was standing at the door as if he expected his number to be called at any second.

At virtually any other time in my life I would have treated this as a comic moment, but there was no comedy in me. At my office I hadn't been working, only sitting at my desk, worrying. Yet I snapped at Rocky for pulling me away from my job.

"I didn't tell them to call you," he said. "How can blood be too old? If it still works, it's good."

"They're not gonna take any from you," I said. "Let's go."

He wouldn't budge. "I told them to test a little from my finger," he said, "to see if it's good enough."

"I talked to the nurse. They just want you to go home. . . . Please, I don't have the strength to argue with you now."

He let me guide him to the door. Before he left he said, as loudly as he could, "If you don't want people to give blood, don't say you do on the television."

I waited with him at the bus stop. "Debby doesn't need blood," I said. "Her blood's fine."

"It can't hurt to try."

"The doctors know what to try."

"Like hell they do. She's getting worse and worse. When you talk to the doctor ask him to give her some blood."

When the bus came, I held his elbow as he climbed the stairs, but he pushed my hand away.

I did speak to the doctor that night, but not about blood. He was with three other doctors and clearly in a hurry.

"I don't have any new information," he said. "All the test results will be in by next Tuesday." We made an appointment to meet at the nurses' station on Debby's floor at three that Tuesday.

During the entire time of Debby's illness only one part of my life had stayed the same. Every day at noon I ran with Huey, a Chinese physicist who also taught at the university. While stepping over tree roots, we looked for shade and whenever possible a water hose.

Huey was a much better runner but kept my pace, so he always had the breath to answer my endless physics questions. He had some problems with English, but in three miles he could explain an electron microscope or Yang's theory of broken symmetry or even everyday things that I would store up to ask him. For me our runs were like combining gym and science.

After the exercise and shower we drove a few blocks to the Cultured Cow and ate tuna sandwiches. The run and shower and lunch altogether took us an hour and a half.

It was a precious part of my day. Huey, who was doing experiments in biophysics, knew what was happening to Debby; he also knew the constant repetitions of her problems didn't help. "Try to think about something else," he said, and he could make me do so at least for that hour and a half.

But during that late spring as Debby faded, I couldn't talk about anything else. I told Huey, and he listened. He tried, when there was an opening, to switch to another subject or at least a larger one, from Debby's brain to the brain in general and all that we didn't understand about memory and knowledge, but I couldn't listen. I didn't care about anyone else's brain.

"Why doesn't she ask to talk to the kids?" I wanted to know. "Why doesn't she know what show she's watching on TV?"

"Wait until the doctor explains to you," Huey said. "Don't try to understand it by yourself."

On that Tuesday as I awaited the doctor's explanation, Huey left for Ireland to attend a physics conference.

At the gym I took my wire basket to a locker as I always did, unrolled my towel shorts and socks, waved to the people who worked at the desk, and headed for the street. I only ran a few steps. The three miles that I covered every day seemed as impossible that Tuesday as running to California. Without someone to talk to I had only the constant dialogue about Debby in my head. I was imagining the doctor telling me what was wrong and what he would do to correct it. I wrote the lines, I saw Debby sit up to shake his hand. Then she called Jessica and Sam and laughed and then called Marcy to ask her to bring an Orange Julius when she came to visit.

"Too hot for you today?" the woman at the desk asked when I walked back inside.

"Yes," I said.

I had those three hours to wait. I had planned to run longer than usual, eat my tuna sandwich, watch volleyball or fencing class or whatever was going on in the gym until two-thirty, and then walk to the hospital complex.

Instead, I got into my car and drove. I had no destination in space, only in time. I had to get from twelve until three. Somewhere along Main Street I parked. Downtown Houston looked absolutely foreign. Lawyers, bankers, clerical workers, and well-dressed people hurried past me on their way to air-conditioning. I wandered into Foley's, a six-story department store. Debby and I had been to their suburban stores but not to the big downtown original.

In the men's department I roamed past healthy-looking mannequins poised for fun, but their lifeless eyes were what I noticed.

"You want to try it on?" a sales clerk asked me. "The dressing room is over there near the elevator."

I was holding a yellow shirt. I followed her toward the dressing rooms. I pulled the curtain and removed the straight pins. The crisp shirt softened in my hands, the cardboard fell out, exposing all that was hidden, the cloth to cover belly and arms. I tried to refold it so that it would look as it had on the shelf, small and precise, all chest and collar, a bright yellow thing separate from the body. I couldn't refold it the way it had been, so I handed it to the clerk, lumpy and with the plastic bag on top. I had the straight pins in my hand and gave her those as well.

"I'm sorry," I said. "I can't put it together."

"It's okay," she said. "You want to try another?"

I didn't dare. Everything seemed too complicated.

In electronics I watched thirty TVs. In furniture and draperies I walked through colonial bedrooms and Danish modern dining rooms, past reclining loungers and end tables, pleased by the order and cleanliness of each room. I could have moved into any one of those decors.

I spent a long time at the Hello Kitty collection—Jessica's favorite. On all the objects a red-and-black kitty almost smiled. She decorated watches, pens, pencils, stationery. I bought a Kitty key chain and held it clamped in my fist like a worry bead.

For at least half an hour I rode the escalator, one to six and then over again. I looked at everything, a two-second view of each floor while I moved to new amazements above and below. I was an astronaut among things that used to be familiar—buttons and sunglasses, fur coats, vacuum cleaners, chandeliers—the world lined up before my passing glance and then slipped away.

I had to force myself from the escalator just the way I had to give Jessica and Sam convincing tugs toward the exit when they were at AstroWorld.

I was better by the time I arrived at the hospital, and I already knew what I was going to hear.

At three-fifteen I sat in the cubicle that belonged to the nursing chief of 5N. Had Huey been there I might have asked him some key questions—how the hot gases became planets, why electrons maintained orbits, whether gravity would ever lose its power and let all things wander disconnected through the universe.

The doctor had just arrived from his own office. I saw him slip on the white hospital coat with his name sewed on in blue. He carried a thick notebook, Debby's chart. I was his first hospital appointment. He had a four-by-six card in his pocket with the room numbers of patients yet to see.

He shook my hand, offered me coffee in a foam cup. He put the chart on the desk in front of him. I didn't know what words he would use, what names he would pluck out of the medical lexicon to tell me what I didn't understand, but by three-fifteen I didn't need him for the bad news. I only wanted directions how to find her.

He opened the chart. "These are the results of the personality test," he said. "They're not as precise as we'd like, but they do show what I suspected. In Debby, the disease has progressed to the point where there's no way to distinguish between her brain and her mind."

"What does that mean?"

"It means that she's not likely to come out of this. We will of course try everything. We'll see if drugs or behaviorism can bring her back somewhat, but I think it's neurological. Her mind can only be what the brain still allows. It doesn't go this way very often."

"Can she get better?"

"Disease is a dynamic process," he said.

He went on to tell me in some detail what was happening to the sticky white covering of Debby's nerves, but the word *dynamic* had thrown me. It seemed so positive. Debby in a dynamic condition sounded good.

Charles Atlas, the world's strongest man, on the back cover of the comic books that I read in Remes's drugstore, used to advertise dynamic tension. His tanned muscles rippled on the page. "If I can do it," he said, "you can do it. It's this easy." He pressed his hands against one another. That was all you needed, the dynamic tension of the right hand against the left and the left against the right.

I was actually seeing Charles Atlas, a man in his sixties with a big belt buckle proclaiming him the world's strongest man. Suddenly he was very blurred. The doctor reached across the desk to hand me a little gray box of hospital tissues.

"You have a lot to cry about," he said. "I'm sorry. I'll ask the nurses if you can stay here a while."

He closed the door quietly. I saw him talking at the desk. He had left the big notebook, Debby's medical record, but there was nothing in it I wanted to read.

In a few minutes I walked down the corridor to Debby's room. "I went to Foley's today," I told her. "If I'd had one of your credit cards, I would have bought a hundred things. I got this for Jessica."

I held up the key chain with the ceramic Hello Kitty. I put it in her hand.

I pressed the remote control, and the TV glowed. In Iran and Afghanistan and Peru, terrorists gunned people down. In China there were floods, everywhere on earth accidents and murders, rapes and burglaries. In our room only quiet. I kissed her forehead and changed the channel. She seemed asleep as John Chancellor retold the news again, or maybe she wasn't. I didn't know how to recognize the difference.

Chapter 20

Although I hardly wrote anything during those years, I found a fragment called "Anniversary." Here it is.

The children were in bed, the dog had eaten, the only thing missing was the wife. She had been missing for three years. Right before our eyes she vanished.

Sam had just turned three and wore white training pants. He liked to measure his foot against Mommy's; they had the same round big toes and high arch.

Jessica gossiped. At school the girls were joining Brownies, the teachers were enforcing the no cuts rule in the lunch line.

Pieces of chicken stuck to the charcoal grill. Sam spilled the barbecue sauce. We cleaned it with white napkins that stuck to our fingertips. Jessica pretended her red-and-white hands were monster claws. She scared Sam off the Yellow Pages, which he used as his booster seat. They chased one another in and out of the house.

At the sink Debby held a frying pan under water, worked at it with her fingers. Her nails were always just the right length, as if they signed a secret agreement with her meaty fingertips. On a portable tape recorder Jessica was playing the music from *Grease*. She and Sam had seen the movie twice. Jessica printed a fan letter to Olivia Newton John. A John Travolta beach towel decorated our hallway. We had bunk beds for Sam and a canopy bed for Jessica, a king-size mattress, big walk-in closets, a backyard, even a garden with a few tomatoes and grayish green peppers.

We were a family eating barbecued chicken on a Sunday night. In five minutes the children would watch "The Wonderful World of Disney." In three and a half hours I would be asleep, comforted by Debby's smooth back not quite touching me but there on the very next row of a firm innerspring. She was twenty-nine. Her biggest worry was stretch marks and the faint line of hair from her navel that appeared after Sam's birth.

It was a sign, she thought: I'm not so young anymore.

I carried in a big communal finger bowl and pretended I was a very polite Japanese waiter. Jessica and Sam dipped their fingers in the water, then grabbed for the striped dish towel. While she was doing the dishes, while her hands were in the grease, Debby disappeared. The handle of the frying pan broke. Sam and Jessica still watched "Disney." Three years later I came back to clean up the sticky mess.

She disappeared a little at a time. When her balance disappeared I caught her. The grease stayed in the sink; the children watched television.

I hired Clara, a practical nurse. She didn't come when it rained. She told me about her own little boy and her sick momma. She believed that Debby caught the sickness by walking barefoot and stepping on a worm that crawled up to her brain from the sole of her foot.

Clara always wore her rubber moccasins. To protect against night worms, she rubbed alcohol on the bottoms of her feet. I let her try it on Debby, too.

Clara and I looked for the worm. I spread Debby's toes; we didn't see the worm, but as I finished rubbing the alcohol across the bottom of her feet I spotted him following the line of hairs from her groin to her belly button. Before I could grab him he slipped into her navel.

It rained for two weeks, and Clara never came back. I sat beside Debby all day and with a flashlight at night, watching for the worm. It never came back either. The children watched television.

I hired a nurse with sharp white fingernails to stab the worm.

I called the doctor, who told me worms did not cause the disease.

The long-nailed nurse left, too. There was no worm, and she grew tired of listening to the children watch television.

Sam was four and in playschool. Jessica could read and cook a little. Every night she crushed Wheaties and poured honey over them. We ate pizza and Wheaties wham. I put away the flashlight and stopped looking for the worm.

"What's the matter with Mommy?" they both asked. "Why can't she talk?"

"Mom doesn't know what to say," Sam said.

Debby left behind two pairs of glasses and her soft contact lenses. In her white wedding gown, with those sad eyes and little fingernails, she went outside to feed the dog. On her way she stepped on a worm.

"There are no worms in our family," her mother said.

As she spoke Debby floated by, carrying the dog's dish. He ate only hard food, so his teeth would not desert him. Debby too had good teeth. She ate no junk food. She disappeared before she had a cavity.

Chapter 21

*J*essica and Sam slept at Bashy and Rocky's house every Saturday night. Bashy pushed twin beds together and joined her grandchildren in a slumber party as they watched "Love Boat" together. Sunday mornings Rocky walked them home and the fighting began.

Sam watched cartoons nonstop. "Transformers" was his favorite show, but he watched "Tom and Jerry," "Bugs Bunny," "Flintstones," and "G.I. Joe," anything that was nonhuman. Between the three UHF channels he had all-day coverage. Jessica wanted to watch baseball.

"You always let him hog it," she complained.

Sam had his standard reply: "She can listen to the radio. There's no cartoons on the radio."

Rocky tended to side with Jessica, I think because he liked baseball, but he made it sound as though it were only for her career.

"She has to watch," he told Sam. "She'll be an announcer someday."

"She can be a radio announcer, too," Sam said.

I missed a lot of the battles while I was at the hospital, but I could see that Rocky didn't know what to do. He tried half measures—giving each an hour—but that satisfied nobody. The cartoons didn't all run on the standard hourly schedule; sometimes an hour left Sam stranded in a plot. Even worse, a mechanical hourly shift could leave Jessica having to tune out with the bases loaded.

"Maybe I'll just buy another TV," I told Rocky, "a small black-and-white."

"It won't help," he said. "They'll fight over who gets the color. What you should do is get the little one away from the cartoons."

I knew he was right, but I didn't have the energy to make any changes. The cartoons kept Sam occupied; that was enough.

"It's a shame," Rocky said. "PeePee needs the television. She tells me what they're gonna do next. She could be the manager."

He called her PeePee, his version of Fifi, her own name for herself when she was a toddler. Fifi stuck, Sam and I still used it, but PeePee was only Rocky's.

He was right about her, too. She followed the games closely; not only the games, she followed innings. On her notepad she put little gold stars beside the ones she wanted to narrate to me.

Sometimes when I would come home from the hospital at eleven or so and open the refrigerator to look for something quick to eat before I went to bed, I would hear her door open. "Can I come out, Daddy?"

She asked first, and I always knew I should say no, but I was so happy to hear her voice that I rarely did. Instead we went through a little charade.

"Is it important?"

"Yes."

"Can it wait until morning?"

"I guess."

She'd start to close her door, then give me one last chance—a burst of information.

"We lost in the eleventh. I want to tell you about it. Then I'll go right to sleep."

Baseball was working for both of us. I did want to hear the details. For some reason, although I'd lost my taste for almost everything else in the world, the fate of the Astros each day held my attention. It was another pennant drive, my first since Kerner was shot before the Tigers' series.

"Five minutes," I'd whisper, and that was all I allowed, but those five minutes redeemed the day. With good news she was almost breathless.

"Slow down," I'd say, "or Rocky won't think you're gonna be an announcer. Then he'll start to get on you for following the Astros and wasting your time."

"He gives me more than five minutes."

"Okay—shoot."

She held her notepad and read from it. She had her own code, a shorthand of X's and Y's for each of the teams. She didn't know how to keep score; instead she wrote out a narrative of what happened in every inning. I only let her read me the exciting innings—when runs scored or there was a great play. She didn't write out the great plays. She just drew a star on that spot in the text and told me from memory.

"Of course I didn't see it," she often added. "Your son was watching 'Richie Rich.' "

Her five-minute sports report did more than bring me up to date, it brought me back. Every day I hurried home, had dinner with Jessica and Sam, then at six-thirty drove back to the hospital. Rocky, Bashy, or the baby-sitter, sometimes all three, put the children to bed.

Sam went to bed early but woke up at night between two and three. He didn't ask permission, he just sprinted down the hall to my room. At first I'd walk him back and tuck him in again, only to have him return in a few minutes.

I gave up. I put an old mattress at the foot of my bed. He stopped waking me; he slept there like a pet. In the morning I stepped over him and went out to pick up the paper. I read about the Astros first, enjoying another version of what Jessica had already highlighted.

There were lots of wins that summer. The Astros had great pitching, Nolan Ryan, Joe Niekro, and a solid bullpen. They hit singles, stole a lot, and played tight defense.

So did we. Jessica defended herself with baseball, Sam used cartoons. For me the best defense was order.

I had a schedule. I could comb Debby's hair and try to feed her and hold her hand and read the paper aloud. That ritual became my office and my home. As much as Debby, I settled into a small room in Methodist Hospital with a fourteen-inch TV, an adjustable bed, a tray table, and an excellent reading lamp. A room near fast elevators and with a drinking fountain at either end of the hall. It was cozy in its way, even romantic. We were more than alone.

Everything else in my life, my students, my work, even Jessica and Sam, were off stage, in the wings. I waved, I threw kisses. I checked in. I read stories at night, paid the baby-sitter, bought the groceries, but the only intense life I had was in that hospital room.

To accommodate us, Rocky had changed his schedule. He took his naps when I was home so that he could be alert when I was at the hospital. While the children and I ate pizza followed by Wheaties wham, he snored on the brown corduroy couch. I hardly spoke to him; our waking hours didn't cross. I would shake his shoulder about six-twenty and have a cup of coffee ready, which he drank while watching either cartoons or baseball.

I was about to buy a second TV when Huey, during one of our runs, had an idea.

"I have a broken one," he said, "a nine-inch. It jumps all the time." He showed me with his hands.

Jessica and Sam both complained, but I stored our twenty-one-inch color set in my office and installed the vertically disordered black-and-white.

Rocky had to close his eyes as he listened to the news. Jessica switched to radio, 100 percent. When there was no baseball she listened to 99Q—preteen rock—but Sam continued to watch TV.

"Doesn't it bother your eyes?" I asked him.

"Yes," he said, "but I still know what's happening."

For about a week he continued his day-long TV vigils. Then, Rocky told me, he started shutting off the TV himself. He still watched his favorites, but he transferred some of his attention to the hallway.

As a fourth birthday present Marcy and her family bought him a set of racing cars, two- and three-inch speedsters that operated on push power. I added to his models a gray Plymouth like the one that I drove.

I noticed that he played with the racers in the hallway. Lots of evenings as I was leaving I had to step over his parking lot to get to the door. One day in July I heard something. He was on his knees, making an engine-revving noise with his throat. I kissed the top of his head, the straight soft brown hair so much like Debby's.

"See you in the morning," I said.

I was already out the door when he stopped revving his Chevy.

"You never play with me," he said.

"I heard that," I said. I pushed the mail slot open with my finger so he could see me. "I'll play with you more soon."

"When?" he asked.

"Pretty soon, you'll see. . . ." I walked fast so I wouldn't hear any more questions before I started my own engine to drown him out. As I backed away from the house I saw his eyes following me through the mail slot.

I was already at the hospital garage and had taken my punched card at the automatic gate. It was too late to turn around. I drove through and paid fifty cents to exit. I drove fast.

When I got home it was seven-fifteen and I walked into the Indianapolis Speedway. All the cars were lined up at one end of the big hallway. Sam knelt beside them. At the other end of the hallway, sitting cross-legged on the floor, his back against the wall, Rocky waited. He held his cap in front of his legs—a target for the cars.

Jessica, taking a break from baseball, kept score here. She listed each vehicle—Fiat, Chevy, Oldsmobile, truck—and kept track of how often each one sped directly into Rocky's cap.

"What's this?" I said. "Sam and his pit crew?"

"Be careful," Sam said. He slid quickly to his left to keep me from stepping on his cars and upsetting the order of their sprints.

I sat down to join him. "Can I play, too?" I asked.

He didn't answer, he just slid back toward the wall to make room for me. His shoes and socks were off, his little toes squeezed the floorboards. He was all business.

"Are you gonna push or catch?" Jessica asked. She was already writing me into the notebook. "Pushing is more fun," she said. "Rocky's always the catcher."

"I'll push," I said, "but you'll have to teach me the rules."

I kicked off my shoes and sat down. I picked up one of the golden Pontiacs.

"Be careful," Sam said, "that one can really go."

"It's not the best one," Jessica said. "The pickup truck gets to Rocky even faster."

"Let's see," I said. I pushed the golden racer, and it sped straight across the floorboard into Rocky's cap. "Mazel tov," he said.

"You didn't think I could drive straight?"

"I didn't think you could think straight."

When he started to stand up he had to get on all fours first and hold on to the wall. Jessica and I ran to help him.

"Now you catch," he said. "I'll sit on the couch."

"Have you been catching cars every day?"

"No," he said. "Sometimes he bounces those little Super Balls into my cap. The cars are easier to stop."

Sam ran to his closet to get his Super Balls. "I've got a whole collection," he said. Vaguely I knew it, but I hadn't sat down with him to appreciate all the colors and sizes. Some came from gumball machines, others he bought or found.

While Rocky rested on the couch I played Super Balls. We measured the bounce of every ball in Sam's collection.

Rocky went to sleep, the baby-sitter left. Jessica brought out her Barbie dolls and treated me to a fashion show.

That evening I was their special guest. Sam went deep into his closet, brought out all the collections—some were his exclusively, others they shared—rubber bands, plastic margarine cups, colored paper clips, disposable spoons, marbles, the paper flowers from get-well cards. They had salvaged what they could. In the hospital room I felt that Debby and I were stranded on an island, but as I examined and appreciated their plastic and paper and rubber and glass treasures, I began to understand who the stranded ones really were.

That night there were no baths. Sam fell asleep in my arms at nine, Jessica snuggled into my lap and sucked her thumb and combed Barbie's hair until ten-thirty.

Chapter 22

*O*nce I missed that first night at the hospital, it was easy to miss others. I still spent my afternoons in Debby's room, but the evenings belonged to Jessica and Sam and, when he chose to join us, to Rocky.

He hated indoor baseball, but for PeePee he went to the Astrodome. I taught her how to keep score the official way, but, sitting with her family in center field, she became more a fan and less a statistician. Sam carried his plastic mitt and awaited five-hundred-foot home runs on every pitch. Rocky complained about the National League.

"They give Polacks a chance in the American League and Italians."

"So does the National League," Jessica argued. "So do the Astros."

"Who they got from Poland or Lithuania?" he asked.

"Terry Puhl," Jessica said, "is from Canada."

"Canada," Rocky said. "Canada doesn't count, it's the same thing."

"Well, who's the American League got from Poland or Lithuania?" Jessica asked.

"Nobody," he said, "that's what's wrong with baseball."

In August, while the Astros and Dodgers jockeyed for the division lead, I began to realize why Jessica had become such a fan.

It wasn't only Rocky and me; the other regulars in our house were also sports nuts.

Joel, Debby's cousin stopped by every day, sometimes more than once. He was twenty-four, a salesman and single. Jessica and Sam liked to go to his apartment because he had cable TV and a cigarette and candy machine, the result of a bad investment. Jessica admired the way he could watch separate games on each of his two TVs and occasionally even listen to a third. Jessica impressed him, too.

"I've never seen anything like it," he said. "She doesn't forget a time at bat. If I had a memory like hers, who knows? I might go to graduate school."

At his house, Joel paced the floor during crucial parts of a game; at our house, Rocky wouldn't stand for it.

"Sit down," Rocky said, "or get out."

Usually Joel was happy to get out; he couldn't sit still for more than one close inning.

The other regular, David, was Jessica's former kindergarten teacher. After the slide show he became one of our closest friends. Jessica still called him "Mister" from his days as her teacher—Sam changed it to "Sister." As soon as David came into the house, Jessica and Sam went for his comb and his wallet so they could hide them, but they settled down for ball games. Rocky made everyone hot chocolate. When I was still going to the hospital every night, if I came home early enough, I'd find everyone in front of the TV—Jessica taking notes, Joel holding the remote control so he could click on other games, David watching the game while he played cars with Sam, Bashy trying to straighten out the kitchen, Rocky snoring from his spot on the big red chair.

"Except for Bashy and the baby-sitters, she's surrounded by men," I told Rocky, "and all she hears is sports talk. I want her to be interested in other things. She's eight years old, she should do what other little girls do. If Debby were here, she'd do things with her."

"You're right," Rocky said. "I'm gonna take her shopping."

A few days later Jessica came home wearing a flowered dress and a bonnet. She ran into her room. "He embarrassed me so much," she said.

"I didn't want this stupid dress and hat, but he liked it so I let him buy it. It was a lot of money, too, twenty dollars."

"Don't worry," I said. "I'll pay him back."

"He won't let you. He took his handkerchief along—if I knew he was going to do that, I'd have never gone. First he told the saleslady that it was way too expensive and asked her when it would be on sale. Then when she said it wouldn't be, he counted out his money right to the penny and then knotted the handkerchief up again. Everybody was watching."

"That's nothing," I said. "Probably nobody even noticed."

"They did, too," Jessica said, "and then he called me PeePee in front of everybody. 'PeePee, let's go,' he said. I'm never going to go back to Penney's."

"Let's make a list of some other things you'd like to do. Maybe you want to go to some plays."

"I want to go to ball games—that's enough."

"What about going to the movies with your friends or roller-skating?"

"Nobody roller-skates."

"Well, they must do something. Ask the girls at school—I'll drive you. How about bowling?"

"I don't like any of that."

"I just want you to play with friends. You used to."

"I don't have any friends," she said.

I started naming them. "Hilary, Ilana, Rebecca, Sarah . . ."

"They used to be my friends. They're not anymore."

"Why?"

"I just don't like them."

"Do they ask you about Mom?"

"Sometimes," she said.

"So it's hard for you to talk to them?"

She nodded.

"I know," I said. "It's hard for me, too."

I didn't press her that day, but I did what I'd been considering for some time. I telephoned a psychotherapist.

Over the phone I told Joyce as briefly as I could what had happened to Debby.

"I know Jessica's lonely," I said, "and I know there are things I can't change, but I want to help her—I hope I haven't waited too long."

Later that week Joyce spent two hours with me at her office, then she went to the hospital to see Debby and check the medical record. By the time she met Jessica she was ready. She took Jessica to Pizza Hut and then drove her home. Joyce was talking to me when Joel came running into the house holding a napkin as if it were a hundred-dollar bill.

"You won't believe this," he yelled. "Look what I got for you."

He opened the napkin on the floor—held Sam back to keep him from trampling it. "To Jessica," it said, "Joaquin Andujar." Andujar was one of the Astro pitchers, an erratic right-hander.

"He just wrote his name at first," Joel said, "but I asked him to make it personal. He was at McDonald's just sitting there with his own kids. He's on injured reserve for two more weeks."

"Are you sure it was really him?" Jessica asked.

"He signed his name—look. Anyway, do I know Joaquin or don't I? Excuse me," he said, noticing Joyce for the first time.

Jessica explained who Joaquin was. She brought out a baseball card and compared signatures to convince herself that it was really Joaquin. She and Sam both examined the napkin like detectives. They agreed it was real and gave Joel high-fives.

"Go back to McDonald's and get one for me, too," Sam said.

"I'll get you Jose Cruz one of these days," Joel said. "Gotta run."

Rocky kept his eye on Joyce. "Are you a doctor?" he asked.

"No," she said, "a psychologist."

"There's nothing wrong with PeePee," he said. "Her father is the one who's nuts."

Joyce stayed an hour and a half. The next day in her office she suggested that both children begin therapy. Sandra, her partner, would take on Sam.

"Is there anything really wrong?" I asked her. "I know it's a stupid question, but I have no perspective. If they can walk and talk and think, it seems like everything is pretty good."

"Jessica has had a big loss," Joyce said. "It's harder to cope with than a death because there is no finality. She doesn't know what she's supposed to do."

"She told you all that?"

"Not exactly," Joyce said. "It's more indirect, but it's pretty clear that she's depressed. Look."

She showed me a crayon drawing Jessica had made. "She did this when we were in her room."

I looked at the drawing. A black horse ate black grass. There was a black flower and a black cloud.

"She told me it was the black stallion," Joyce said. "You don't have to be Sigmund Freud to figure out how she feels."

"Why is she so stuck on baseball?"

"It gives her a way to reach you," Joyce said, "a neutral way, a way not connected to Debby or anything else. Baseball is a straight shot to you."

"She wants to hang around with me all the time. She'd quit school if she could."

"Of course," Joyce said. "She doesn't want to let you out of her sight. It's almost like an infant's fear that Daddy will never return when he leaves the room. Jessica calms that part of herself with baseball. While you're gone she's got that, so she's not afraid."

"I guess it makes sense."

"It's a long, slow process," Joyce said. "Jessica has had a terrible blow losing Mommy like this—she'll have to learn to trust the world again so she can let go of you and baseball."

"What can I do to help her?"

"I can't say for certain," Joyce said, "but from what I've seen, I'd guess you've got some letting go to do as well."

Chapter 23

*J*oyce had two specific suggestions, a cat and Brownies, the junior Girl Scouts. I resisted the cat, Jessica vetoed Brownies. She also tried to convince me that seeing Joyce was a waste of time.

"She's not fun to play with," Jessica said, "and she always asks me 'How do you feel about this?' and 'How do you feel about that?' Why is that her business?"

"That's her job," I said, "finding out how you feel and helping you to understand your feelings."

"I understand how I feel without her," Jessica said. "All she does is snoop around."

"She's trying to help. Give her a chance."

"When she asks me how I feel about my mom, I ask her how she feels about her mom."

"Does she answer?"

"Does she ever. She talks the whole time, and you're paying for it. I don't even listen. If you really wanted to make me feel better, you'd fire her and buy season tickets with the money you'll save."

She'd guessed right to remind me of the cost. Jessica had two appointments a week with Joyce, Sam three with Sandra. Once a week the two therapists met with me. Rocky called them the big babies.

"Grown-up women like those two," he said, "sitting on the floor and playing games . . . they should be ashamed of themselves."

"Why?" I asked. "You do it, too."

"I don't get paid, it's not a job. They should know better."

Sandra and Joyce both agreed about the cat.

"She's lonely and she loves cats," Joyce said, "and we can learn a lot from the way she relates to the cat."

"Can't we learn just as much from the way she relates to George?"

"I don't think so," Joyce said. "George is the family pet, not really hers. I think she needs to connect to something that's completely separate from everything else that's going on."

"I'll think about it," I said. George convinced me more than the psychologist did.

I knew what bothered the dog. He looked everywhere for Debby. He crawled under the bed and tore open the garbage bags full of spices, all we had left from our store. He howled in the kitchen. In the yard he uprooted the azaleas and dug into soft places in the ground as if he could find Debby if he went deep enough.

I tried to take him to the hospital for a visit and went as far as asking our doctor, who didn't like the idea, before I stopped trying to get permission. I considered sneaking him in, but I knew George would bark like crazy when he saw her. The closest we came was one Sunday afternoon on the hospital lawn. Jessica and Sam and Rocky held him on a leash, and I brought Debby to the window. The children waved. George looked around.

"He wants to see you," I told Debby. "He's been looking everywhere."

We were five floors up, but Jessica and Sam could see us. I pressed my face against the window. Jessica held George by his paws so that he stood on his hind legs. Rocky kept trying to keep the leash from getting tangled in Sam's feet. People walking past smiled at the scene. I could read the children's lips as they called out to Mommy. Hearing that word must have made George bark. He bounced around on his hind legs. Sam helped Rocky hold tightly to the leash.

"George is going nuts. He wants to see you. Can you wave?"

I held her hand in the air and pressed it against the window. I supported her in that position for a minute or two—long enough for everyone to wave and throw kisses to her.

Three weeks earlier the doctors had switched Debby to psychiatry to see if anything in that department could help. They gave her drugs that made her sleep and caused her body to become rigid. When that didn't help they decided on behaviorism.

"It's worth a try," the psychiatrist said. "If she is in charge of any of her behavior, the reward system might pay off."

"She doesn't ask for anything," I said. "How can you reward a person who doesn't want anything?"

"We'll deny some of the things she's getting now, then give them back if she responds."

"Like what?" I asked.

"You're the one who knows that best—try making a list. I'll go over it with you."

We started by denying Debby her mail. Every day I brought something from the children.

Jessica had just switched from her careful printing to rounded cursive letters. She wrote notes to her mother, decorated them with flowers and trees and birds. The colors were bright, the words were what they had to be: "Get well, fast," "I love you," "I miss you."

I didn't tell the children that under the doctor's direction I was now withholding Jessica's letters and Sam's drawings. I kept them in a bag at my office. Debby didn't respond, but her room, without the children's decorations taped to the wall, lost its only brightness.

As another experiment in denial, I stopped reading aloud, and the room lost its sounds. Nothing else changed. When the doctor asked me if I'd consider cutting off my visits for a while, I refused.

"You're probably right," he said, "but let's give it a few more days."

When we stopped the experiment I taped all the letters and drawings that I'd collected to the wall beside Debby's bed, and I decided to bring George, my own experiment.

When I came downstairs to the lawn near one of the parking lots, the dog was loose and about to attack a security guard. He wanted to find Debby. George had bared his teeth. His backbone stiffened. The security guard had removed the billy club from his belt and held it in his right hand.

"Don't hit him," Jessica yelled to the guard. Rocky tried to get the leash back on, but George was too quick for him. He kept moving away, circling ever closer to the guard.

I saw what was happening as I ran out of the building. I grabbed George's collar, but he snarled and tried to fight me off. He went after the guard. Before he got there I kicked him in the ribs. When he fell to the grass, I grabbed his choker and pulled as hard as I could.

"Stop it, Daddy," Jessica yelled. Sam held on to Rocky. George tried to bite my hand so that he could get to the guard. I grabbed the leash and tied it around his jaws like a muzzle, then, still holding his choker chain, I pulled him toward the car. He was shivering and so was I.

"That's a mad dog," the guard said. "I would have shot him if the kids weren't here. If I were you, mister, I'd have him put away."

In the car we had to wait a long time until George was calm enough for me to begin driving.

"Would the policeman really have shot him?" Sam asked.

"I don't think so," I said. "It wasn't the policeman's fault, he was just standing there."

"George doesn't like policemen," Sam said.

"That's not why," Jessica said. She had her hand on George's head and opened the window a little so he could hold his nose out and sniff the air. Rocky, sitting between the children, watched to make sure the dog's wildness didn't return.

I waited for Jessica to continue. When she didn't, I asked, "Why do you think he was so angry?"

"Because," Jessica said.

That night I called Joyce and okayed the cat. On Saturday she arrived with Snow, a white Siamese whose previous owner had given her away because she couldn't be housebroken. Joyce didn't tell me that. By the time I figured it out it was too late—Jessica already loved her.

"Okay," I told Jessica. "I gave in on the cat, you can compromise on Brownies."

"I'm not going," she said. "I don't have to do everything Joyce says."

"It's not only Joyce. I want you to go."

"You're just saying that."

"I'm not . . . I think Brownies will be good for you. I wish I'd thought of it."

We were sitting in a red vinyl booth at the Pizza Inn. Rocky drank coffee and kept his eye on Sam, who liked to push the buttons on the jukebox.

"You think everything she says is a good idea. You're always on her side."

"She's right," Rocky said. "You don't need those women to play with the kids. Let them get a real job."

"And he's always on your side."

Jessica smiled.

"But let's get back to Brownies. What have you got to lose by giving it a try?"

"I don't want to," she said, "and you can't make me." She left her slice of pizza half-eaten and walked to the car.

"Leave her alone," Rocky said. "Why do you bother her with clubs?"

"Just don't try to talk her out of it."

"I don't even know what it is," he said.

"It's Girl Scouts for younger girls."

"Like what you did? The Cub Scouts? You didn't have enough yourself, now you want it to happen to PeePee?"

He stormed out of the Pizza Inn to join Jessica in the car.

"I know why Rocky doesn't like Girl Scouts," Sam said. "It's because they make cookies, isn't it?"

Chapter 24

*T*he Brownies, of course, also met in a church, St. Anne's. Jessica went to the meeting only because I bribed her. After the meeting I promised I'd take her to a ball game.

"Is Nolan Ryan pitching?" she asked.

"He's scheduled."

"You can watch at home free," Rocky said. "Why do you want to throw away money?"

"All right," Jessica said, "I'll go to Brownies, but only if we get to stay for the whole game, even if it's extra innings."

Rocky stayed with Sam—I didn't tell him we were going to a church—but I wore a hat, my blue Astros cap with an orange star.

The troop had already been meeting throughout the school year. We were late. When we entered St. Anne's recreation room, the girls were sitting in a circle. Kay Randall, the troop leader, held her hands out from her chest. She looked at her fingernails as if she were checking to make sure they were all the same color.

"Take a deep breath," she said. Twenty Brownies inhaled.

"Ready?" Kay Randall asked. She didn't wait for an answer. "Close your eyes," she said, "and bridge."

Kay continued to breathe deeply as she put her fingertips together. The girls imitated her. Jessica and I sat on folding chairs and watched.

"Let's get out of here," she whispered.

I ignored her.

After about thirty seconds, Kay stood. "Five-minute break," she said, "a quiet one." She came over to us. I had spoken to her on the phone. She shook my hand and Jessica's. Then she held Jessica's hand and walked her across the room to join the other girls, who were eating Ritz crackers and drinking half-pints of milk through colored straws.

"I know we're joining late in the year," I told Kay, "but I hope Jessica can still benefit from being part of the group. She knows most of the girls."

"Of course she can," Kay said. "Not everyone has to start at step one—it's not the army."

I looked over at Jessica, sitting with the group. She held an unopened carton of milk.

"She tends to be a loner," I told Kay. "The group might help."

"We have a lot of shy girls," Kay Randall said. "Scouting brings them out. Believe me, it's hard to stay shy when you're nine years old and you're sharing a tent with six other girls. You have to count on each other, you have to communicate."

I imagined Jessica zipping up her sleeping bag, mumbling good night to anyone who first said it to her, then closing her eyes and hating me for sending her out among the happy.

"She likes baseball," I told Kay.

"There's room for baseball in scouting," Kay said. "Once a year the whole district goes to a game. They mention us on the big scoreboard."

"Jessica listens to most of the games. She's a real fan."

Kay smiled.

"That's why I want her in Girl Scouts. You know, I want her to go to things with her girlfriends instead of always hanging around with me."

"I understand," Kay said. "It's part of bridging." She put her fingertips together again. "It's what we were doing when you came in."

"I wondered what it was," I said. "I thought it had to do with drying nailpolish."

Kay smiled, raised her fingertips to eye level. "This is a bridge," she said, "a symbolic one. There are five levels of scouting, and we bridge between each one. These girls are coming close to the end of their Brownie experience. In the fall they'll be junior Girl Scouts. Bridging is a way to get ready for what comes next so it won't be so scary."

She raised the whistle that hung around her neck, blew one short blast. The girls returned to the circle.

"Are we gonna do projects now?" one of the girls asked.

"No," Kay said, "we'll finish bridging, but first let's welcome Jessica." The girls held hands and swayed from side to side. "Hello, hello," they sang. "Hello to Jessica." She sat on the floor between Sarah and Rebecca. Kay raised her hands, and twenty girls in white shirts and brown sashes held out their stumpy chewed fingertips and made bridges. Jessica kept her hands at her sides.

When Kay lowered her arms the circle broke up and the girls went to a long table where buttons of all sizes were laid out. There were also rubber-tipped bottles of glue and thick paper.

"Crafts," Kay told me. She helped the girls get started. Jessica participated. She picked an assortment of buttons and began to arrange them into a pattern.

"Decide what you want before you glue," Kay warned, "and try not to get too much on your fingers."

While the Brownies glued buttons I eyed St. Anne in her grotto and St. Gregory and St. Thomas. Their hands were folded as if they'd started out bridging and ended up praying.

During the break, when Kay asked me if I could help out, I volunteered.

"Katherine's mom helped all year," she said, "but they moved to St. Louis a month ago. It's kind of hard for one person to get all the things together every week. But if you're too busy . . ."

"I can do it," I said. "One night a week is okay."

After the meeting, while I helped Kay carry the supplies to her car, Jessica walked a straight line to our Plymouth. She didn't jabber with any of the girls, didn't linger, just went right to the car, strapped in, and braced herself for destruction.

I waited until the sixth inning to say anything about Brownies. Nolan was throwing nothing but smoke and had only given up an infield single through six. In the program Jessica was looking for a particular statistic, how many one-hitters he'd already pitched. I tried to give her my new information in the best possible moment, while Nolan still looked great.

"I'll be going to the Brownies' meetings, too," I told her. "I volunteered to be Kay's assistant."

"You're off your rocker," she said. "I'm not joining. I'm never gonna go again."

"What have you got to lose? They have fun. You'll get to do things, go on field trips . . . and next year you can go right into Girl Scouts."

"Girl Scouts is stupid," Jessica said. "Who wants to sell cookies and glue buttons and walk around wearing stupid old badges?"

"All right," I said, "suit yourself, don't go. But I said I'd be an assistant and I will."

"I know why you're doing this," Jessica said. "You think that because I don't have Mommy, Kay Randall and the Girl Scouts will help me. That's crazy. And I know that Joyce is supposed to be like a mother, too. Why don't you just leave me alone." She shut the program and laid down her scoring pad.

In the seventh Nolan gave up four hits and a walk. In the eighth he came out for a pinch hitter. Although she had made me promise to stay into extra innings, Jessica wanted to leave.

In the morning, she told Rocky that I had joined the Brownies.

"You don't have enough on your hands," he said, "you got to join clubs."

Jessica smiled as she ate her cereal.

"I made a commitment," I said, "because it's a good organization whether Jessica agrees or not. If she doesn't want to learn things, I still can."

"Sure," Jessica said, "go ahead. Learn how to make a necklace out of safety pins and paste colored tissues into stupid designs."

"Nobody's forcing you," I told Jessica. "You do what you want and I'll do what I want. A promise is a promise. I signed up to be a leader, and I'm going to do it with you or without you."

"But you didn't even ask me if I liked it. You just signed up without talking it over."

"That's true; that's why I'm not going to force you to go along. It was my choice."

"What can you like about it? I hate Melissa Randall. She always has a cold."

"Her mother is a good leader."

"How do you know?"

"She's my boss. I've got to like her, don't I? C'mon, honey, give it a chance."

"If you make me go I'll do it, but if I have a choice I won't."

Every Tuesday Rocky stayed with Jessica and Sam while I went to the Brownies' meetings. We talked about field trips and how to earn merit badges. The girls giggled when Kay pinned a promptness badge on me, my first.

Jessica thought it was hilarious. She told me to wear it to work.

Sometimes when I watched Jessica brush her hair and tie her ponytail and make up her lunch kit, I started to think that maybe I should just relax and stop the therapy and the Brownies and all my not-so-subtle attempts to get her to invite friends over. I started to think that in spite of everything, she was a good student and she had a sense of humor. She was barely nine years old. She would grow up as everyone else did. My Cub Scout model, John Clark, did it without a father; she would do it without a mother. I started to wonder if Jessica seemed to the girls in her class the way John Clark had seemed to me: dignified, serious, almost an adult even while we were playing. I admired him. Maybe the girls in her class admired her. But John had that hero on the wall, his father in a uniform, dead for reasons John and all the rest of us understood.

My Jessica had to explain a neurologic disease she couldn't even pronounce. "I hate it when people ask me about Mom," she said. "I just tell them she fell off the Empire State Building."

Chapter 25

*A*fter the changes and behaviorism failed to change anything, the hospital started to pressure me. Sharon, from their counseling office, came up to see me one morning.

"Can I buy you a cup of coffee?" she asked.

I suspected what it was about. Sharon had come up a few times before. She was a woman in her mid-fifties whose hair had gone past gray to white and cushioned her long face. Understanding oozed from her. She reminded me of the good-hearted neighbors in movies, the ones who come over after the fire and, without asking, begin to help you rebuild the barn.

Until she came into the room I had been feeling pretty good. It was my morning for Sam's carpool. He didn't sit next to me on the front seat, he wanted to be in the back with Kevin and Brad. Two months of therapy, a broken TV, and fifty or so hours of rolling cars in the hallway had made a difference.

"The staff doesn't think you've faced everything," Sharon said.

"The staff," I said, "can shove it."

"I'm glad to see you express some anger," she said. "It's very appropriate, but the anger won't solve anything. You have a big decision coming up."

"Is that what the staff meeting was about?"

She nodded. "We've talked about this before. I know you're trying to avoid it. I don't blame you. It's your decision, of course, but I've compiled a short list of nursing homes. . . ." She handed me a packet.

"They're for old people," I said, "not for Debby."

"They're for people who need them," she said, "at any age."

I shook my head. "How much longer can she stay here?"

"At the meeting," Sharon said, "we decided that she could be released immediately—but she can stay until you've made other arrangements—up to ten days. Sometimes," she said, "a person is so close that they don't see."

"I see," I said. "It's one thing to see, another to do."

"That's true," she said. She handed me her card. "I have an appointment now, but anytime you want to talk some more please call me. Maybe if you visited some of these places, you might change your mind."

Sharon was wrong. I hadn't avoided the issue. I thought about nothing else.

I had talked to the medical people and to Joyce and Sandra and briefly to the director of the Jewish Home for the Aged.

"For Debby," one of the nurses told me, "it may not make that much difference, but you'll have to be comfortable with whatever decision you make."

I had the pamphlets Sharon left for me in a manila envelope when I drove up to our house. Sam and Rocky were shining shoes. Rocky sat on the lawn chair. He splattered Shinola liquid onto Sam's white canvas shoes. He put the polish on the laces, too. Sam, holding the brush, waited for the shoes to dry.

The trash cans were at the curb, the animals' dishes clean, the driveway swept. Jessica came running out with a message.

"When Sandra dropped off Sam she said you should call her as soon as you get home."

"I'll call her," I said, "but I need my hug first."

When she felt like it, Jessica added to my hug a bonus, a little tickle with her long hair against my cheek. She refused a haircut, and long wavy bangs obscured her lovely face.

Joyce had a psychological explanation. "She's trying to hide behind the hair. Lots of kids are like that. She's a little extreme, but don't fight it."

I didn't. I bought her a cream rinse and a detangler, which she sprayed on without much effect. When her curls got too knotted I just snipped off a chunk.

When I reached Sandra she was still at her office. "I'll wait for you," she said, "if you can come over right now."

Only two months earlier I'd had to drag Sam, literally howling and kicking, into her office. Now he looked forward to seeing her and sometimes chose the games he wanted to play with her the night before.

She was a tall, slender woman, almost too glamorous looking in her high heels and hose to be on the floor playing with Sam. Rocky told me to watch out. She might be a kidnapper.

She laughed out loud at that one and had been patient and kind to Sam even when he was hysterical and throwing toys at her. She usually made me feel better about Sam. This time she didn't.

Harriet had been in town for the weekend. She had taken Sam and Jessica to Toys "Я" Us and loaded them with gifts.

"Sam told me about his grandma's visit. Do you know what they did?"

"I think so," I said.

"Did he tell you they went to the hospital to see Debby?"

"Yes."

"Did he tell you what Grandma did?"

"I don't think so," I said.

"She put him on Debby's lap and told him to kiss Mommy and that would make Mommy better. Then she told him that Mommy did talk to her and told her what to say to the children. He wants to know why Mommy can talk to Grandma and not to him."

"She wants it so badly," I said, "that she's making it up. She doesn't mean any harm."

Sandra lit a cigarette. She knew I didn't like smoke and apologized. "She may not mean any harm," she said, "but she sure can do some. If

I had to come up with a scenario designed to create psychosis in children, this would be it. They're getting the message that it's their job to save Mommy, and now they've got a translator, someone who understands Mommy and knows what Mommy wants. Have you told the children how bleak Debby's condition is?"

"They know."

"But have you told them?"

"Not in exact words, but we always talk about it."

"I think it's time," she said, "to put all the cards on the table. Sam is already worried that he can't save Mommy and that Grandma is going to be mad at him. I asked Jessica about what happened, and she told me the same story."

"I can't stop Harriet from saying what she wants."

"If you can't," Sandra said, "who's going to protect your children?"

———·———

We went to the coffee shop at Penney's. It seemed like the right place. The children were there so often with the baby-sitter that the waitress called for two cheese sandwiches as soon as she saw them walk in. Rocky came, too. Because the restaurant wasn't kosher, he drank only water. He didn't complain that I let the children eat cheese sandwiches there, but I think he would have been angry if I had eaten one. He didn't have to worry. I had no appetite.

I told Jessica and Sam about my conversation with Sandra, and I reassured them that Debby wasn't talking only to Grandma Harriet.

"If she could talk, she would talk to you guys. The other thing you have to know," I said, "is that you didn't make Mommy sick, and you can't make her better. No matter how much you want to, no matter how much you love her, you can't make her better."

"Who can?" Jessica asked.

"Nobody."

There were only about a half dozen tables in the coffee shop, and at a few minutes before the six o'clock closing we were the only customers.

"The doctors can't do anything else?" Rocky asked.

I shook my head. I hadn't told him so directly, either. The children ate their sandwiches.

"I've known for a few months that Mommy's not going to change. The doctor told me, but we still wanted to try everything, in case there was a chance."

"Why didn't you tell us?" Jessica asked.

"I wanted to protect you a little longer. I should have told you."

"I knew it," Sam said. "I knew Grandma Harriet didn't really talk to her."

We lived only six blocks from Penney's. When we got home I gave Sam an early bath because he was streaked with dirt from the park. When I dried him, I saw the curve of Debby's toes in his. I put him into his Green Hornet pajamas. He carried Snow around in his right hand, chanting, "One-handed Snow." The cat purred to the rhythm.

In the backyard I saw Jessica. She was picking up pebbles and throwing them. She wound up like Nolan Ryan but threw the pebbles straight up into the air.

Rocky had gone outside with her and dozed on a lawn chair a few feet away.

I watched her throw the stones, one by one taking aim and then firing with all her might. She owned a mitt and a Whiffle ball and a hard rubber ball and lots of tennis balls. I picked up my glove and a tennis ball and went outside.

"Wanna play catch?" I asked.

She shook her head.

I squatted like a catcher. "C'mon," I said. "You can be Nolan Ryan and throw all fastballs."

She shook her head again.

"I'll chase the ones that get away," I said.

She shook her head again. She wasn't just idly flipping the stones, she was concentrating hard, the way she did when she printed her letters carefully. She was working. I watched her aim at the sky and throw a half dozen more. It was starting to get dark and looked like rain. I wanted to wake Rocky and get his lawn chair into the house.

"Aiming at something?" I asked.

Jessica nodded.

"What?" I asked.

"God," she said.

I watched her throw for a few more minutes. The little stones fell back close to where she stood. She was getting tired. I could tell by how quickly they came falling back. I came over and picked one up. We took turns. I threw mine as hard as I could, too. When it started to rain we woke Rocky and went into the house.

Chapter 26

When Jessica stopped going out for recess, Mrs. Klein called me in for a conference.

"I don't force her, of course," Mrs. Klein said. "I make sure it's what she really wants, then I offer her the use of the library, or even the cafeteria. If she wanted to read instead, I wouldn't be surprised; that happens from time to time. Not all eight-year-olds love to play. . . . But Jessica doesn't want to read or have a snack. She just takes out those cards and thumbs through them. I thought you should know."

"I know," I said. "She does it at home, too."

"She's explained to me what she does," Mrs. Klein said, "but I'm not a baseball person, so it doesn't make much sense to me."

"She's updating the statistics on the cards. It's probably my fault," I said. "I taught her how to figure out batting averages so she could enjoy long division, and now she keeps track of everything. I'm batting one ninety-eight on cleaning the kitchen."

"It may be a useful hobby," Mrs. Klein said, "but missing recess coupled with her lack of interaction with the children throughout the day . . . you know, it worries me even though I understand the situation."

"I'm aware of it," I said. "She sees a therapist, and I'm trying to get her involved in Brownies."

"I'm sure you're doing everything you can. I just feel so sorry for the little sweetheart."

"She doesn't need you to feel sorry for her, Mrs. Klein, that's the last thing she needs. Please treat her like you do everyone else."

"I do, of course," Mrs. Klein said. She spoke crisply when she saw that I was annoyed, but I could tell by the way her voice quivered that she was giving Jessica plenty of pity.

"My son kept up with baseball cards," Mrs. Klein said, "but he was thirteen or fourteen. Isn't she too young for it?"

"I've taken her to a lot of games, and she listens every day."

"I know," Mrs. Klein said. "I've warned her about listening during class. You've seen the note."

"I have, and I back you one hundred percent. She's not allowed to take her radio to school."

"I'll just continue to monitor the situation," Mrs. Klein said, "and we'll hope things get better. She's an excellent reader and speller, and the math, well, with all that practice I guess it's no surprise."

Joyce, unable to connect very well to Jessica in spite of the cat and twice a week pizza, decided to try a ball game, too.

"I'll never do that again," Jessica said. "If I have to do something with her, I'd rather go to her office and play Boggle."

"She warned you," I said, "she's not a fan."

"She talked all through the game."

"Not everybody likes to concentrate on each pitch," I said. "Joyce just went for the entertainment."

"She went to spy on me."

"It's not spying. She tells me everything she notices, and she tells you, too."

"Well, she doesn't notice much. There was a triple and a wild pitch in the fourth, and all she noticed was that my Coke was empty. I hope you didn't pay for her ticket."

"Maybe if you go to some more games with her, she'll learn."

"Nope. If I don't go with you, I'd rather listen."

Joyce called it separation anxiety. "She's keeping score, literally, so she'll know where she stands."

Once, when Jessica begged and I couldn't go, I let Rocky take both children. I dropped them at the north entrance and arranged to pick them up at ten.

"Unless it goes extra innings," Jessica said.

"Ten," I insisted, "even if they play all night. And make Rocky take the escalator, don't let him walk up the ramps."

"Don't tell me where I can't walk," Rocky growled.

Jessica gave me a look that told me not to worry, she'd be in charge. She knew how to handle him. When he missed part of a game because he dozed off she could narrate the action almost exactly as Larry Dierker called it on the radio. Sometimes she gave him extra pleasure by putting in details especially for him.

"Cedeno's going back, back, and he catches it with his back against the wall, four hundred and fifteen feet away in straightaway center and Joe DiMaggio would have caught it with his eyes closed, and nobody paid him a fortune, either."

At ten, the three of them were waiting at the north entrance. Sam ran to the car. "Nobody had any home runs, and we lost," he said. "Rocky bought me a sign." He held up an orange Astros pennant.

"They charged three dollars for that," Rocky said. "For three dollars you can eat for a week."

"Why'd you buy it, then?" I asked.

"He wanted it."

"He doesn't have to get everything he wants. You're a soft touch."

"They argued about it until the fifth," Jessica said, "then they walked to ten different stands."

"I thought it would be cheaper up high," Rocky said, "where there's not so many customers."

"It cost three bucks at every place," Sam said. "It's not fair."

"A nickel's worth of material," Rocky said.

"As soon as they came back to our seats they both fell asleep," Jessica said, "and before that Sam kept asking me the score every five minutes. I woke them at quarter to ten. It's no fun when you're not there."

For her ninth birthday, I surprised Jessica. I invited all the girls in the class, fourteen of them, to the party. Jane, one of Debby's best friends, brought some tapes. I pretended that we were going to the movies to celebrate—on our way I turned back because I forgot my wallet. Through the rearview mirror, I kept my eye on Sam. He never let out a peep.

When we walked in, the girls were all hiding in the bedroom. On the table was a surprise for me, too. I expected a birthday cake.

"You like it?" Rocky asked Jessica.

"It's so beautiful," she said, "I don't think we should cut it." She ran over to hug him.

Rocky had made her a three-decker wedding cake. Instead of a bride and groom he'd put the figure of a ball player on top. She was still hugging him when the fourteen girls ran out yelling, "Surprise!"

I was sorry the minute I saw the look on her face. The cake was plenty. When Jane put on the tape and all the girls went to the living room to dance, Jessica went to her room. Rocky followed her.

"Is she coming out?" Jane asked me.

"I don't think she liked the surprise. Go ahead, entertain the rest of them." When I knocked at her door Jessica was lying on her bed, facing the wall. Rocky rubbed her back.

"I thought you'd like a surprise party," I said. They were dancing to her favorite song, "Bette Davis Eyes."

"I didn't want a party. I just wanted to go to the movies like you said."

"Do you want me to send the girls home?"

"I don't care, they're not my friends."

"They sure sounded like they were, they were all excited to come . . . and you," I said to Rocky, "you pulled the biggest surprise of all. Why didn't you tell me what you were baking?"

"Because you'd say no."

"That wouldn't have stopped you."

Jessica smiled. "Is that the kind of wedding cakes you used to make at the American Bakery?" she asked.

He nodded. "I made them bigger, but I couldn't get the forms around here. The brides used to make a lot of money on my cakes. At Polish weddings everyone would get a slice of cake and a dance with the bride

and then pay for it. That's the way they gave presents. And the more
drunk, the more dances and slices of cake. Sometimes I'd go to the
weddings and the bride would tell me, 'Rocky, you shoulda baked me
two cakes, I'd be rich.' "

"Are you gonna come out to cut it?" I asked. She looked at
Rocky.

"Sure she'll cut it," he said. "A cake is to eat, not to look at."

Jessica washed her face. When she and Rocky walked to the cake,
the girls stopped dancing. They came down the hall as if he were walking
her down the aisle. She wore blue jeans and white Keds and a striped
sweater, but the cake made her as much a bride as a birthday girl.

The dancers sang "Happy Birthday" quietly, and everyone stood
near the cake. Rocky had arranged nine candles on the second tier, and
the one to grow on at the top next to the ball player. "Be careful," Sarah
said when Jessica took a deep breath, "don't get any spit on it."

I cut. There were more than enough flowers for everyone. Jessica
gave the first piece to Rocky.

"You'll make one for her wedding, too," Marcy said.

Rocky gave her a mean look. "Her wedding isn't my business."

"I'm sorry," Marcy said. "I only meant to say that you've made her
a birthday cake as beautiful as a wedding cake. When it's Dalia's birthday
can I pay you to bake one for her?"

"No," he snapped. "I don't bake this for anybody, not anymore,
just for PeePee."

Every girl took a big piece. Sam ate three flowers, and there was
still three-quarters of the cake left.

While I talked to the mothers as they arrived to pick up their girls,
Rocky cleaned up. When everyone left and I began to help, Rocky
covered the third tier of the cake in aluminum foil. I pulled the foil apart
to look at it; the ball player and the candle were gone, but the white
fluting on the sides and the frosting were untouched.

"Take it to Debby," Rocky said.

While he continued to pick up plastic spoons and wipe away ice-
cream spills, I kept my eyes on the cake. It was ten years late and missing
the bride and groom, but he hadn't only baked this cake for a birthday.

I said that to Debby when I put the cake on the table in front of her. "Rocky told me to bring you the crown," I said. "I think he's trying to tell us he wishes he had baked it for our wedding."

I held the white frosted circle up to her face. I put a bit of the frosting to her lips. She made no attempt to eat any. I tried again with a piece of the cake, then I wiped her lips clean and cut the cake into four for the duty nurses.

Chapter 27

*I*n October the principal called. Mrs. Klein caught Jessica in spelling class listening to the World Series through an earphone.

"It's against the school policy," Mrs. Simmons said. "Jessica understands school policy. We confiscate radios and send the child home."

Rocky took the call. "She has spelling every day," he told the principal. "The World Series is only once a year."

"I've called her father at his office, but I haven't been able to reach him," Mrs. Simmons said. "Is there anyone else who could pick her up?"

Rocky walked the five long blocks. When he got to school, Jessica was sitting on a bench outside the principal's office. The confiscated radio was on Mrs. Simmons's desk.

Rocky took Jessica's hand. "Where's the radio?" he asked.

Jessica motioned to the door marked "Principal."

"He knocked," Jessica told me later. "He didn't just walk in and yell at her. Anyway, I don't think she understood him, so I told her what he was saying."

Rocky wanted the radio.

"I'm sorry," Mrs. Simmons said, "the radio has been confiscated. She can have it returned after a seven-day period."

"By then she won't need it," Rocky said. "The Series will be over."

"That," Mrs. Simmons said, "is exactly the point."

"I bought her that radio," Rocky said. "I've got the receipt to prove it." He fished it out of the zippered change purse that the children and I bought for him last Father's Day.

"Nobody is taking the radio. It's hers, she just can't use it for a week."

"Are you in the union?" Rocky asked.

"I am a member of the teachers' union."

"Is that where you learned to steal, or were you a crook before you joined those robbers?"

"I tried to pull him away then," Jessica said, "but he wouldn't move."

"Give her the radio," Rocky said, "or I call the Labor Department. You union people think everything is yours—jobs, radios, you can't even leave a kid alone to listen to the World Series."

"Not in school."

"She learns more from the radio than from the school. She'll be an announcer someday."

When he grabbed the radio from her desk, Mrs. Simmons didn't try to stop him. He pulled out the earphone and turned up the volume, high so he could hear. The voice of Vin Sculley and then a Gillette Foamy commercial blared into the halls.

Mrs. Simmons followed them out the door. "Her father will hear about this, and so will her teachers."

"Good," Rocky said. "I'll tell all the people I know, too."

When Mrs. Simmons did reach me, I went right to school. By then she was calm. She knew Jessica less well than the teachers did, but she went out of her way to let me know that she wouldn't hold Rocky's behavior against Jessica.

"I know it's her grandfather, and I tried to reason with the gentleman," Mrs. Simmons said, "but he had no respect for school policy."

"Actually," I said, "he's her great-grandfather, and he doesn't have respect for very many policies, but I apologize for anything he said or did."

We agreed that Jessica would stay home from school the next day to reprimand her.

When I came home and broke the news, Jessica screamed with pleasure. "I'll be able to watch the seventh game!"

"You see?" Rocky said. "The principal knew she was wrong."

The Brewers were Jessica's favorite American League team. She liked Rollie Fingers, and especially Robin Yount.

"Does Yount go in the hole better than Harvey Kuenn used to?" she asked me.

"You bet," I told her. "Kuenn was never a great fielder, but he could hit three hundred with his eyes closed."

Kuenn was the Brewers' manager. He had an artificial leg and could barely make it up the dugout steps, but when I was Jessica's age and the Tigers were my team, Kuenn used to stand at the plate, tap the corners with his bat, spit some tobacco juice, and knock liners up the alley.

She rooted for the Brewers even though Joaquin Andujar, whose autograph she had Scotch-taped to her wall, now played for the Cards.

On the morning of the seventh game it was eighty-five in Houston and our air conditioner didn't work.

"Good," Rocky said. "Now we can watch the game in peace."

I decided to wait until spring to repair the air conditioner and spent some time on the phone trying to price a fan that would cool two rooms and the long hallway. When the seventh game began Jessica had the starting lineups in front of her on three-by-five cards.

The Braves wouldn't win, Rocky insisted, because they didn't have a Polack.

"Polacks are home-run hitters," he said. "Kluzewski, Yastrzemski, Luzinski . . ."

"The Cardinals don't have any Polacks, either," Jessica said.

"But they had Stanley Musial."

"Was he a Polack?"

"Yes."

"How do you know? He doesn't sound like one."

"Everyone knows. They called him Stashu . . . that's his Polish name."

They were still arguing when the phone rang.

"If it's the school," Jessica said, "I'm still being punished."

"It's probably someone calling back about the fan."

I had a pencil in my hand and a piece of scratch paper near the phone so I could write down the model number and price.

"I'm at the hospital," my caller said. "I'm taking Debby out. If you want to see her, get here right away."

I knew Harriet was coming, though not the exact date. A week earlier, when I made my decision, she made hers, too.

We were now enemies, a situation Debby would have approved. It started when I phoned Harriet after I told the children what Sam called "the whole truth." I told her she had to stop confusing them.

"You can believe whatever you want, hope for whatever you want, but don't tell Jessica and Sam things that are only fantasies. They have to know what's real, it's the only way they can face it without ruining their lives."

"So," she said, "you're joining the doctors and the witch doctors and giving up on your wife."

"I'm trying to protect our children, that's all. They know the truth— don't confuse them."

"The truth," she said, "is that the doctors have made her worse. As soon as she gets home she'll be fine. The children will make her better."

"No, they won't," I said. "Children can't cure this kind of disease. You can't put that pressure on them."

"She'll come home and everything will be fine. I'll hire people to take care of the house and the children. If you can't take it, you leave."

A few months earlier I wouldn't have argued. But now I knew, not because of what the doctors said or what Harriet demanded. I knew from Debby.

For almost three years she had fought the good fight. Partial vision and half a bladder and shaky limbs and the devastating dizziness had not overwhelmed her. But in the last six months, something had. I didn't know what to call it, but I couldn't pretend that there was still a Debby who understood.

"I'm making arrangements," I told Harriet, "to move her to the Jewish Home."

"Never," Harriet said. "My daughter will never be in a home."

"It's not a prison. If she gets better, she'll come home. I talked to the director. They have a young woman there now in similar condition. They're being very helpful."

She knew my weakness and went for it. "You didn't put the old man into a home," she said. "How can you put your wife there? She's not like those old people."

It was true. Debby wasn't like them. On the day I visited, I envied most of the retirees. They played checkers, went on bus trips, complained about their meals. Debby would be housed not with them, the director told me, but in the hospital section. I was no happier about it than my mother-in-law, but I didn't know what else to do.

I had told Jessica and Sam that Grandma Harriet would be coming to Houston to take Mommy to her house for a while. They were prepared, and I thought I was, but my hand shook at the phone.

"How much is a fan going to cost?" Jessica asked. The game was in the middle of the fourth.

"It was Grandma Harriet," I told her. "She's come to take Mommy to Michigan." I picked up my car keys.

"You want me to come?" Rocky asked.

"Stay with Jessica," I said, "and wait for Sam's carpool. I don't know for sure how long I'll be gone."

Jessica put down her pencil and scorecard.

"You don't have to go," I said. "You just saw Mommy on Sunday, nothing's changed."

"I still wanna go," she said.

Neither of us spoke on the drive to the hospital. I pretended I was listening to the game. I thought Jessica was paying attention.

"What's the score?" I asked when we pulled into the garage and there was too much static to listen.

"I don't know," she said. She held my hand in the elevator. The door to Debby's room was open when we arrived. Harriet was pushing back into the room a steel cart filled with hospital toiletries. The paper slippers hung from the side of the cart like ears.

"She doesn't need any of this," Harriet said. "She has all her own things at home."

Harriet had brought a helper with her, a woman in her twenties. She didn't speak to me, but she hugged Jessica and then introduced her to the attendant. Harriet was exceptionally jovial. She had dressed Debby in a red-belted dress, one I had never seen.

The attendant stood by, not sure what her role was supposed to be. "You'll see," Harriet told her. "In a week Debby will be doing everything herself. And will she ever let us have it if her canopy bed isn't in her room just like it used to be. This morning that was the first thing she asked me about."

Jessica looked at me. She knew it wasn't the truth. She looked at me for help, but that afternoon I couldn't give it, I needed help myself.

An orderly pushed Debby's chair down the hall. Harriet and the attendant followed, and Jessica and I trailed them.

Outside, Ben waited in a rented Buick. He nodded to me and waved to Jessica. The attendant, taking my job, helped Debby into the car, then they strapped her onto the front seat. Jessica and I approached the car.

I leaned down so I could kiss Debby's cheek. I smelled her perfume, saw the rouge and lipstick.

"Come kiss your mother," Harriet said. Jessica leaned her face quickly toward Debby.

"Kiss her," Harriet said. "You won't see her for a while, but she'll get well fast at Grandma's house."

Harriet and the attendant went inside to get the packet of medications that they'd forgotten in the room.

Debby stared straight ahead. Ben kept the window rolled up so the car would stay cool. Jessica and I looked at her through the glass.

"Mommy doesn't wear lipstick and makeup," Jessica whispered to me. "Why did they do that?"

"Grandma Harriet wants her to look good."

"But Mommy doesn't like it. Make them take it off."

"You're right," I said, "but I don't want to get into an argument about it. Let them do what they want. It's not hurting her."

"It's not fair," Jessica said, "just because Mommy can't stop them."

We waved until the Buick was out of sight. At our car, we forgot to turn on the radio. We stopped at Sears to pick up the fan. I bought the biggest one they had—a fifty-eight-inch oscillating model that sounded like a hurricane.

"With that baby you're gonna blow your house off its foundation," the salesman said. "You sure you want one that powerful?"

"I'm sure," I said.

I paid in cash and had fifty dollars left. I gave it to Jessica and told her to buy anything she wanted.

"Whenever you're sad, Daddy, you want to buy me things." She put the money back in my hand. "It won't help."

At home I had no energy even to take the fan out of the box. I carried it in and left it for Rocky and Jessica. Nothing had changed. Debby hadn't been home since late spring, but that afternoon I couldn't stand to stay indoors. I sat on Rocky's aluminum lawn chair watching the tennis courts across the street. There were only two courts in the park, and they were filled most of the time.

Debby and I would lie in bed at night sometimes, reading, our toes touching, almost asleep, while tennis balls from across the street softly hit the cement. "Fault," she would say if I dozed and the book fell to my chest.

Rocky came out. He carried a paper cup full of ginger ale, his version of medicine. Whenever he didn't feel well it was the first thing he asked for.

"I'm okay," I told him.

"Drink it anyway," he said. "You'll be more okay."

"Daddy," Jessica called through the mail slot, "are you coming in?"

"Pretty soon," I said.

"Sit," Rocky said. "I'll take care of her. When the carpool comes I'll take Sam, too."

I drank the ginger ale. I could tell time was passing because there were at least three different sets of players on the courts before I stood up to face what was the whole truth—my life without Debby.

As soon as I opened the door I smelled the aroma. Jessica was standing on a chair holding the star cookie cutter. She licked chocolate chips from her fingers.

"Do you believe it?" she said. "Rocky's helping me bake cookies."

The erstwhile cake man, his sleeves rolled and flour up to his elbows, had three sheets of stars and one of chocolate chips cooling on the Formica counter. I smelled more in the oven.

"We'll have enough for a bake sale," Jessica said. "When Sam gets home we can set up a table outside. Shall we charge a dime apiece?"

"Too much," Rocky said. "A nickel is plenty."

When the carpool dropped Sam off, Jessica and Rocky had already carried the coffee table to the curb. Jessica was laying out Toll House cookies on white paper towels. Sam ran right to the sale table.

"Rocky baked cookies," he said. "How come?"

I took out two nickels, bought one from Jessica and one from Sam. Though the bitterness at the back of my throat did not leave then or for a long time after, on that day I still could taste the sweetness. Lots of cars drove past without stopping. They didn't know what they were missing.

Chapter 28

*I*n Kay Randall's den the leaders of troops numbers 114 and 226, and Kay and I were planning the Brownies' final event, a day-long picnic and flower gathering at a ranch. It was a seventy-mile trip, and we tallied supplies for the busload—three troops, three leaders, the driver, and me, the assistant. Kay, like Anne and Terry, the other two leaders, had been on the same outing numerous times.

"The girls will all pretend they're glad to leave Brownies. They'll try to get their uniforms as dirty as they can," Kay said, "but every one of them, years later, will still have her little notebook of pressed flowers. That's why I keep going on these ridiculously long bus trips. It's a big event for them."

"It's kind of sad for me every time," Anne said, "the year of bridging, it's like the last time they're still kids. That's why I stop at Brownies— Girl Scouts is already like Junior League or a sorority."

Kay gave me the easiest job, cold drinks and snacks for sixty-two. The other leaders would take care of supplies and parental permission forms.

"Jessica is welcome," Kay said. "Even though she hasn't joined, she might still want to go on the picnic."

"Believe me," I said, "I've invited her."

"Please tell her that I'd like her to come. Would it help if I called?"

"I don't think so," I said. "At least for now I'm the only Scout in the family."

"I admire you," Kay said, "for sticking with it, even though Jessica rejected it. She might get something indirectly through your experiences."

"I don't know about that," Terry said. "All my husband says he gets from Brownies is cold suppers."

We were sitting on the colonial furniture in Kay's wood-paneled den, doodling on our supply lists. Kay poured coffee, we traded stories about our troops. . . . It felt so ordinary that I could hardly believe I was part of it.

"We have to be sure that the girls understand that the bluebonnets they pick are on private land and that we have permission to pick them. Otherwise," Kay warned us, "they might pick them along the roadside, which is against the law."

I imagined all sixty-two of them behind bars for picking bluebonnets and Jessica laughing while I scrambled for bail money.

"Are you going on to Scouts?" Terry asked.

"Don't press him," Kay said, laughing. "It's too hard to find a replacement."

"I haven't decided," I told her. "It depends on how things go at home. . . . For now, I think Brownies is my limit."

"Maybe you'll change your mind at the ranch," Terry said. "The bridge there is really nice. It's probably more important than the wildflowers."

In the past few weeks, when the girls put their fingers together to bridge, I joined them. Bridging reminded me of the meditation classes Debby and I had gone to. In the instructor's apartment the seekers closed their eyes and said "om." The instructor told us "om" was the sound of the universe humming through eternity. I always felt silly trying to sound like the universe. Bridging was quiet, just an awkward pose of nine-year-olds uncertain about what would happen next. I felt like one of them.

At home, I showed Jessica. "I'm bridging," I said.

"So is everyone in my class. It makes me sick."

Rocky was sure it was a form of paganism. "You put your fingers together and then go out in the woods to pick flowers. Maybe that's good for you. PeePee is too smart for that."

"The picnic is the last event," I told her. "Next semester they'll be Girl Scouts and you'll be in a different school. You used to like picnics."

"I'd go with you and Sam and Rocky," she said, "but who wants to go with all of them?"

"You can't always hang around with us," I said. "Sam is already spending a lot of time with his friends, and I have to work."

"Then I'll hang around with Rocky."

"You can't hang around with him all the time."

"Why not?" she said. "You did."

"If Rocky goes on the picnic, will you go?"

"He'll never do it," she said.

I thought she was right, but I gave it a try.

He answered with a simple no and went back to reading his Yiddish newspaper. "It's important," I said. "If you go, maybe she'll go, too."

"She can pick flowers and get sunburned in the park," he said. "I'll go with her."

"The whole idea is for her to go without you."

"So she can go alone. It's just across the street, she always goes there alone. I'll still keep an eye on her."

"I'm not talking about across the street, I'm talking about out into the world to be a little girl, to have a childhood."

"She doesn't need that. She's too smart for all that."

"She's not, Rocky. She's missed years of having fun and playing and just being a kid."

"You think she's the only one who has trouble. In Yagistov there was a big orphanage—kids who had no mothers and no fathers and nobody else to take them, either."

"She's not the only one," I said, "but she's the only one we can do something about."

He held up his newspaper folded into quarters so he didn't have to look at me. "You know what would be the best thing for her?"

"What?"

"A job. I wish she could work days and go to night school."

"She's just nine. Give her a break, she's got her whole life to work, maybe a year or two to still be a kid."

"I can't stand going with a busload of kids."

"You went with me to Chicago."

"That was a mistake, too," he said.

When I was in the sixth grade and no class parent could sign up for our proposed trip to the Museum of Science and Industry, I begged him to do it. It was a four-hour bus ride each way. The sixth-grade science teacher had told us all year about the coal mine right in the museum, and I wanted to go down into it. Rocky and two teachers took us.

He went with me into the artificially damp, dark world of the coal mine. The other sixth-graders and I felt our way along the walls and then in the lighted areas read about the things made from American coal and about mining disasters.

On the ride home while we all sang "Ninety-Nine Bottles of Beer on the Wall," Rocky, swaying with the motions of the bus, chanted the evening prayers in Hebrew. We drowned him out.

"All right," he said. He put down his newspaper. "I'll go, but I won't pick any flowers."

Jessica was more stubborn. "I don't know how you tricked him," she said, "but I'm still not going."

I was sure she'd change her mind. "Why are you making such a big deal out of it?" she asked when she went to the store with me and helped me load three cases of Coke and 124 lunch-size bags of chips into the trunk. "It's just a dumb old picnic."

"You're right," I said, "it's not so important—there will be plenty of other trips for you to go on. But we've gotta start someplace."

Until picnic morning I expected her to come, so did Rocky. He made her a peanut-butter-and-honey sandwich and wrapped some herring for himself in wax paper. All morning she stayed in her room and wouldn't come out. Sam had spent the night at his friend Brad's house and would remain there all day.

"We can't leave her," Rocky said. "I'll stay."

"You said you were coming, I'm counting on you to keep your word."

"I was coming so PeePee would go, not to sit on the bus with your wild gang."

He put his lunch back in the refrigerator and turned on the TV. I went to the phone. Juana, our once-a-week cleaning lady, was home and said she could baby-sit all day. Rocky trusted her.

"She'll be okay with Juana," I said. "You know that."

He didn't answer. A few minutes later he took his lunch out of the refrigerator, then put it back in. He wanted me to give him an absolute reason to go, something powerful enough to counteract his desire to please his PeePee. If I had a letter, something official from a doctor or a pharmacist or my boss, he would have been satisfied. He liked facts, not theories.

When Juana arrived he stood up and reached for his change purse. I held his arm.

"You're gonna give her fifty cents for her trouble and tell her to go home, right?"

"A dollar," he said.

He pulled his arm loose from my grip, unzipped the coin purse, and took out a folded bill.

"All right," I said. "If you're too lazy to go on the trip, stay home— I'll do it alone."

"What do you have to do?"

"You know what I have to do, the cases of Coke, the potato chips, all the food other people are bringing, you think a picnic is easy? The girls will be playing, somebody's gotta do the work."

When Jessica came out of her room I showed her the waffles in the waffle iron. Rocky picked up his lunch and went out to the car.

"If you want anything else, just ask Juana."

"Juana doesn't speak English."

"She understands, that's enough."

"Maybe for you it's enough."

"Honey, I told you, you can come; there's plenty of room on the bus. It's not too late for you to change your mind."

"It's not too late for you, either. There's going to be other leaders there. You don't have to go. You're just doing this to be mean to me. And taking Rocky is supermean."

I was ready for this. I had spent an hour with Joyce the day before, steeling myself. "Before she can leave you," Joyce said, "you'll have to show her that you can leave. Nothing's going to happen to her. And don't let her be sick that day, either."

Jessica was too smart to pull the "I don't feel good" routine. Instead she became silent. She stayed in her pajamas. When I left, she didn't say good-bye.

Rocky didn't talk to me on the trip, either—he looked at his watch lots of times and then pulled his cap over his eyes to nap. When we got to the ranch I grabbed the heavy cases of Coke. He handed me the potato chips, then stayed on the bus with the driver while I ran out into the field with the Brownies.

I caught up with Melissa, Kay's daughter. She stood under a tree, tears streaming from her eyes.

"Melissa," I said, "it's okay. Brownies is over, but Girl Scouts will be even more fun." I offered her some of the raisins I carried.

"I'm not sad," she said. "I've got allergies." She sneezed and ran away from me.

I watched Melissa sniffle even more among the wildflowers, and I pointed out the names of various flowers to Carol and JoAnne and Sue and Linda and Rebecca, who were by now used to me and treated me pretty much as they treated Kay. I noticed that the Girl Scout flower book had very accurate photographs that made it easy to identify the bluebonnets and buttercups and poppies. There were also several varieties of wild grasses.

We were only an hour and a half from home on some land a wealthy rancher had long ago donated to the Girl Scouts. The girls bending among the flowers seemed to have been quickly transformed by the colorful meadow. The gigglers and monotonous singers on the bus were now like the bees, sucking strength from the beauty around them.

Everyone had collected lots of flowers by the time Kay blew her whistle. She signaled for us to gather at the bridge, a twenty-foot wooden semicircle that passed above a rocky creek as it ran through the meadow. The bridge was only wide enough for one person to cross at a time, perfect for what we needed.

Terry stood on one side with a paper bag full of Girl Scout wings. The girls were ready to cross. Carol went first. She put down her flowers, stepped to the creek side, and looked into the shallow water.

"Twist me and turn me and show me the elf," she chanted in a singsong rhythm. "I looked in the water and saw . . . myself." Then she walked to the bridge, clenched her fists, and crossed over. On the other side Terry pinned the Girl Scout wings to her collar.

"I will do my best," Carol said, "to be honest, to be fair, to help where I am needed . . ."

The girls were all quiet; there was no pushing in the line. Although it was only midafternoon, some of them held candles.

Rebecca poked my arm and pointed. Far from us, near the gate, Rocky was bending, picking flowers. I backed away slowly so I wouldn't disturb the ceremony, then I ran across the meadow.

I was out of breath when I got to him. "Let me do it," I said. "I don't want you to bend."

He pushed me aside. "Look at you," he said, "running around like a nine-year-old, and PeePee is home. It's upside down."

"You're right," I said. "That's why it has to change."

I walked back to the bus with him, watching from the distance as my troop and the others, one by one, went from elf to winged being.

Rocky and I were on the bus waiting as the junior Girl Scouts marched on, carrying wildflowers.

He was asleep already. I didn't know how long he had been picking flowers before we spotted him. He snored on the bus, the whistles followed by the puffs that had been the music of my childhood. A few of the girls who walked past giggled when they heard those noises coming from the first row, but most were subdued. They were showing their wings.

Kay came over to check. "Is he okay?" she whispered.

"Yes," I said. "You don't have to whisper, he's pretty deaf."

"Maybe the sun was too much for him," she said.

"I don't think so," I said. "It's just his time to nap. He'd do it at home, too."

I believed that, but one of these days I'd be wrong. He was 104, and there was no way to count on anything. When I had taken him for a routine chest X ray before his cataract surgery, I got tense when I saw the doctor look at the film for a long time.

"Is it normal?" I asked.

"I don't know," he said. "I've never seen an X ray for someone over a hundred. I don't know what normal is supposed to be."

On that day, among the Brownies and wildflowers, I knew. I moved the air-conditioning vent as far to the left as it went so the cool air wouldn't blow on him. His cap covered his eyes and moved slightly to the puffs of breath. He didn't wear a jacket, but in the heat and humidity he hadn't even loosened his tie.

Kay stood for a moment just behind the driver. She looked around in the crowded bus, then she bent toward me again. "I want to make an announcement, but I'm sure the whistle will wake him. Maybe if I just stand here for a minute, they'll notice."

Kay put her finger to her lips—it took a minute or two, but the girls became silent.

"I just want to remind you to meet your parents at the south end of the parking lot—they'll be waiting there. They can't drive all the way to the bus stop. . . ."

A girl from one of the other troops came toward the front of the bus, waited until Kay finished her announcement, and then asked me, "Is he really a hundred years old?"

"More than that," I said.

"You can't stand in the aisle," Kay said. "Please go back to your seat."

The girl tore a page of wide-lined white paper from her notebook. "When he wakes up," she said, "would you please ask him if I could have his autograph?"

"I think he's gonna sleep all the way," I said.

"But if he does wake up. . . ?"

"If he does, I'm sure he'll be happy to do it."

I didn't wake him until we arrived at St. Anne's and unloaded. I said good-bye to Kay and to the troop. The driver didn't rush me, he smoked a cigarette a few feet from his bus. I picked up Rocky's cap and pulled on his left earlobe.

He sat up in a hurry and wouldn't let me hold his arm as he stepped down from the bus.

"Thanks for coming along," I said. "I hope it didn't tire you out."

"I'm not tired," he said, "I'm worried about PeePee."

When I opened the door to the house I could smell the taco sauce that Juana had made. Jessica was in her room. I suspected that she had spent the day listless and tearful, although I had asked her to invite a friend over. She came running to the door when she heard us.

"We had a lot of fun, honey, but we missed you."

"The Astros lost five to four," she said. She tried to act as if everything were fine.

"Next time," Rocky said, "you're going, not me."

"No, I'm not," Jessica said. "I hate all of that."

"Then you can try other things," I said. "It doesn't have to be Scouts, but I'm not gonna let up. You can't spend all your time with us."

"Tell him to leave me alone," she asked Rocky.

He handed Jessica the flowers he had picked. "Here," he said. "The other girls all had flowers, so I got you some. I don't know what you're supposed to do with them."

In the driveway, Brad's mother sounded her horn. Rocky went out to claim Sam. Jessica held the flowers like a shield.

"Are you still gonna take me to ball games?" she asked.

"Of course."

"Are you just saying that or do you really mean it?"

"I mean it, but I want you to start bringing a friend along. I mean that, too."

"When you were little and Rocky took you places, he didn't make you bring a friend, did he?"

"That was his mistake." I laughed. "Look at us now, still hanging around together."

"I don't think it was a mistake," she said.

"Maybe not, but guess what—I'm no Rocky."

"I know that," Jessica said, "but when you're real old maybe you will be."

"I'll try," I said, "but I want you to promise something, too."

"What?"

"Try to have fun." She couldn't hold back any longer. She dropped the flowers and cried against my shoulder. I felt like holding her the way I used to when she was an infant, the way I rocked her to sleep. But she was a big girl now and needed not sleep but wakefulness.

We heard Sam and Rocky open the gate to the backyard. George ran to them.

"I'll try," she said. She wiped her eyes. "Don't tell Sam I was crying." She went to the kitchen for a vase. After she'd put the flowers in she turned to me. "I'm going outside," she said.

At the patio door she stopped. "Did Rocky do all that bridging junk?"

"No," I said.

"I knew he wouldn't."

"He didn't have to," I said. "He's done it lots of times. Who do you think showed me how?"

Chapter 29

When he was eighty-nine, Rocky developed a persistent cough. He drank a lot of his usual remedies, ginger ale and hot water with lemon, and when they didn't help he went to the doctor, who prescribed a course of antibiotics. But the cough remained, and the hoarseness was getting worse. It annoyed him enough to return to the doctor. This time an X ray revealed a growth on his vocal chord.

"In that spot and with his symptoms, I'm sure it's cancer," the doctor told me. I asked him to let me explain it to Rocky.

"You've got to tell him the truth," the doctor said. "He's going to need surgery."

"I'll tell him," I said. "I'll just use a different word."

I picked a good one, "boil." In Hebrew it was majestic, one of the ten plagues that God visited upon Pharaoh. In Yiddish, a *geshvir* could be a wart, a pustule, an annoying everyday malady, a distraction, but not a killer.

"If you don't let them take that boil out," I told him, "the cough will never go away."

He agreed to the surgery. "In 1917," he told me, "they wanted to take out my gall bladder, so I said 'Take the gall bladder and anything else that could give me trouble'—and until now I've been okay."

The cough bothered him so much that he seemed to be looking forward to the operation. We were in the Medical Towers parking garage for a presurgical checkup when he changed his mind. I held the passenger door open and was trying to pull him out of the car when a security guard, mistaking me for a mugger, grabbed me from behind and pinned me against the wall. Rocky loved it.

"He's not a crook," he told the guard. "He's a dummy. He believes everything the doctors tell him."

"We have a four o'clock appointment," I told the guard, who still had a grip on me, "and he won't get out of the car."

"Can I accompany you?" the guard asked, and Rocky, suddenly meek as the sweet old guy he was pretending to be, walked alongside the guard directly to the office. I trailed a few feet behind.

"You ought to be more gentle with your grandpa," the guard told me, "he's no problem at all."

A few days later when he was in the hospital and awaiting surgery, I needed help again. The operation was scheduled for eight. He spent the night before in the hospital, and so did I, on the floor beside his bed. He was up at four and was ready. By six he had put away his tefillin and read the paper. We watched the "Today" show. At eight he was barefoot and standing at the door. At eight-fifteen he walked to the nurses' station to ask where the doctor was. The nurses told him it was not unusual for the surgeon to be late.

"He told me eight," Rocky said. "Eight is eight."

By nine he had reconvinced himself that he didn't need the operation. By nine-thirty I couldn't hold him back; he was dressed and about to walk home. I rang for a nurse, but he was down the hall before she arrived. When I blocked the elevator he headed for the stairs. "That doctor's a liar," he said. "I don't want a liar operating on me. I don't need it, anyway—there's nothing wrong with me. I need more hot water with lemon, not an operation."

We were on the landing of five, two flights from where we'd begun, when a nurse yelled down that the doctor was ready and waiting.

"He's a liar," Rocky said.

"He's sorry," the nurse said. I could tell that she was trying not to laugh. Then I heard the doctor's voice.

"I'm very sorry to keep you waiting," he said. "I had another operation, and it took much longer than I thought it would."

"Why?" Rocky yelled up. "Did you make a mistake?"

He hesitated on the landing. His knuckles were white as he gripped the rail. For the first time I saw that he was afraid. I put my hand over his and loosened his grip. Slowly we walked up the stairs.

At the seventh floor, the doctor and his two assistants waited at the top of the stairwell. They waited again outside the room while Rocky took off his suit and put on the hospital gown.

He was still angry when he got onto the stretcher and an orderly wheeled him toward surgery. I walked alongside.

"Do you remember," I asked him, "when I had my appendix out? I was on the stretcher and then you came running down the hall."

"I remember," he said, "I was scared."

"So was I until I saw you."

I was twelve, and after years of teasing me, my quirky appendix one Saturday afternoon inflamed to the bursting point. Dr. Schnorr poked at my stomach and then told my parents to bring me to the hospital.

It happened while Rocky was at the synagogue. When he came home and my sisters told him where I was, he ran to the hospital. When he caught up with me at the edge of anesthesia he was sweating and red-faced and out of breath.

"*Mein kind*," he asked, "are you sick?"

"No," I said, answering him with one of his own phrases, "I'm fine, but the doctors need to make some money." I fell asleep laughing.

"I wish Dr. Schnorr was still alive," Rocky said.

"You have a better doctor, a throat specialist."

"Schnorr knew more about throats than these guys will ever know. He was a throat specialist, too."

When I was sick it was often Rocky who took me to Dr. Schnorr. There were no appointments. You came and then you waited on one of his red leather couches or chairs. Most of his patients were Polish women with bulging goiters in their necks.

Sometimes, when I had tonsillitis or the grippe, I sat in the office, my throat smeared with Mentholatum and then swaddled in washcloths.

With my shirt collar open and the washcloths bobbing around my Adam's apple, I felt a deep kinship with the roomful of women in babushkas waiting alongside me.

The orderly interrupted us. "You'll have to wait out there," he said. I hadn't even realized until I started to back away that Rocky and I were holding hands. He held on and propped himself up on one elbow.

"If I die," he said, "you can have all my suits."

"None of them fit me," I said.

When the orderly wheeled him through the operating room doors, I was smiling.

The next morning, breathing through a tracheotomy tube and un-able to speak, the nurse gave Rocky a toy, a Magic Slate, so he could communicate by writing to me on the plastic page, which erased every time you lifted it. I knew by then that the cancer had been completely removed, but the doctor wasn't certain how much of Rocky's voice would return. He mentioned a mechanical assist for the voice box sometime in the future.

"Can I get you anything?" I asked him.

"Stockins," he wrote, making each letter night school perfect.

I went to the gift shop and bought him the only ones they had, red-and-black argyles. He liked them.

He spoke in a whisper after that—but twice a week for six months he went cheerfully to therapy sessions, where he learned to breathe from his stomach so his voice could be stronger. He didn't need a mechanical assist. His whisper was more emphatic than most voices.

At ninety-seven and again at one hundred there were more "boils," this time in his colon, and this time the word was even more accurate. He had polyps, first one and then three years later another that became malignant.

By calling these cancers "boils" I wasn't fooling myself, and I don't think I was fooling him, either. Each time I explained with a drawing, a snaking intestine with harmless little boils and one big one that choked his bowel.

"Just a boil," I said, "but if you don't take it out, it could kill you."

"You're telling me," he said. "What's a person? A feather. You can die from a toenail. Let's go."

Before the first operation the surgeon had looked grim; afterward, when he told me it had gone well and shook my hand, he said, "The mortality tables will tell you that he should have been dead yesterday or twenty years ago, but I wouldn't bet against this guy."

After each operation Rocky was home in two weeks and fighting me to let him pull the garbage to the curb.

When he was about 105 he stopped walking over to our house, but by then Jessica and Sam were old enough to visit him. Most days, on my way home from work, when I stopped to see him, he was in his usual spot on the front lawn, reading from one of his volumes of Talmud. George still sat beside him, but in his canine old age, he merely wagged his tail at motorcycles.

When Rocky was 106 and his hearing so bad that Sam used to yell directly into his ear, I received an invitation to visit Brazil as a literary lecturer for the United States Information Agency.

Since the onset of Debby's sickness I hadn't written anything. My life had narrowed first to her needs, and then to Jessica's and Sam's. For a few years I had neither the time nor the peace of mind. My storytelling went entirely to the children. Jessica and Sam got five stories a night, all made up on the spot. Sometimes it took me an hour and I left their room sweating, but once in a while when a bedtime story engaged me, I missed my old work.

The invitation to Brazil came at a time when I wasn't getting others. The trip itself wasn't important, but for me it would be a first step, a way to return to my life as a writer. A small uncertain step, as a "speaker," but speaking words that would be my own. Everyone I talked to encouraged me.

"I can take care of the kids," Bashy said, "go ahead." My next-door neighbor Marcy and the carpool mothers, who had become such close friends, gave me confidence, yet as much as I wanted to go, I kept hesitating. Finally, as the deadline for commitment closed in, I realized that it wasn't Jessica and Sam who held me back.

When I sat on the lawn beside Rocky one day in 1982, I was both a forty-one-year-old man talking about a trip to Brazil and a five-year-old boy asking if I could go across the street.

Rocky was not in good shape. He was losing weight. It didn't show yet in his body, but his hollow cheeks made his nostrils seem larger. He had one leg thrown over the armrest of his lawn chair, and he pulled his cap down a little to shade his eyes. I asked, as always, indirectly.

"If I go to Brazil," I said, "can I get you anything?"

I thought he'd dismiss me with a hand gesture and tell me as usual that he didn't need anything. He thought about it for a minute. I didn't care what he said. I waited, not for his words, but for the look in his eyes, his false bravado, his impatience, the signs I had been reading all my life. I would know if my old roommate thought he could give me up for two weeks.

"Maybe you can find me a pair of yellow shoes down there," he said. "Look around."

I did. In Rio and São Paulo and Brasilia, when I wasn't talking to students or being escorted to literary groups, I was sticking my head into shoe stores, looking for yellow size sixes.

The shoes were his gift to me. The way I'd used "boils" to urge him to turn his thoughts from death, he used yellow shoes to tell me that he wasn't going to die while I was on another continent, not if he could help it.

I came back loaded with souvenirs. All the boys in the carpool got five-inch bullwhips, the girls got leather change purses. For Bashy I bought a purse and a lapis necklace, for Jessica and Sam wallets. And in that land of leather, in Recife, a city not far from the Amazon, I found a pair of yellow canvas shoes, size six. Rocky wore them proudly to the synagogue, and a few months later, before he went to the hospital, he put them away in his closet with newspaper stuffed in the toes to hold their shape.

This time there was no further medical help; his entire body was failing. In the hospital we could only wait. Bashy slept beside her father on the vinyl armchair that unfolded into a bed. I prepared Jessica and Sam, told them that Rocky was very, very sick, but they didn't believe me.

On Sunday they came to see him, elated that they were sneaking in even though the hospital prohibited visitors under twelve. An intravenous solution had strengthened him temporarily. When Jessica and Sam came in, he raised the electric bed so that when each of them stood on a stool they could lean over the guardrail to kiss him.

"Your mustache tickles," Sam said. He was almost seven.

"Don't squish his mouth when you kiss him," Jessica said. She took her turn on the stool and delicately offered her cheek.

"Don't forget," he told me, "on Tuesday take out the garbage."

When Bashy took the children to the cafeteria for ice cream, he motioned for me to lower his bed. I leaned over the guardrail, and into his yellowing ear I yelled in words what he had taught me with his life.

"*Shtark zich!*" ("Strengthen yourself!") I yelled it so loudly that a nurse hurried in. I waved her away.

He shook his head, and I put my ear close to hear his whisper, "*Ich ken shein nicht.*" ("I can't anymore.")

He was sleeping when Bashy and the children returned. In the cafeteria Jessica had made a discovery.

"Rocky is more than half as old as America." She showed me her figures on a cafeteria napkin: $1982 - 1776 = 206$. Sam wanted me to double-check.

"It's true," I said.

On the ride home we continued to talk about Rocky's age in relation to America's.

"Did Rocky's father know George Washington?" Sam asked.

"No," I said, "but maybe his great-grandfather could have, if he'd been living in America."

The children seemed dazzled by the idea that their country wasn't even twice as old as their great-grandfather. It made history seem so close. I was thinking about it, too, when a few hours later, as I cooked spaghetti Bashy called to tell me he was going fast.

I left the children with Marcy. In the hospital elevator a sleepy young man handed me an "It's a Boy" cigar. I was holding it when I walked into Rocky's room, just seconds after he died.

Because Jewish tradition forbids embalming and encourages immediate return to the dust, we buried Rocky in Houston, far from his wife and son in Michigan, farther still from his Lithuanian parents.

We buried him in his shroud and his tallith and with his bag of Jerusalem dirt, but on the wooden coffin I poured the symbolic first shovelful of Texas soil and then laid down the shovel to fulfill the role I'd been born to. As his son, I stepped forward to say the Kaddish.

The rabbi held out a book, but I shook my head. I knew the words by heart, yet I was sobbing too much to say them. The small crowd waited, Bashy, my sisters and their families, a few neighbors, some of the old men from the synagogue. I wanted to get all the words right. Rocky didn't like mistakes. "*Yisgadal, v'yisgadash*," I said, almost in a whisper . . . I couldn't go on. The rabbi standing on the other side of the grave asked with his eyes if he should help me, but I shook my head again.

Jessica and Sam, through their own tears, were watching as I took a deep breath and looked up past the solid tombstones and the gardener's cottage, past the supermarket and the auto parts store to the high arc of I-45, where lines of traffic bent toward Dallas and Galveston.

"*Shtark zich!*" I told myself, and I did.

In the land of Washington and Lincoln, on a patch of grass not even visible from the highway, I prayed, thinking of another great American, my little Rocky. My voice steadied, and I made no mistakes. By the last stanza, everyone could hear.

Epilogue

After years of lingering, Debby died in her parents' home.

George the dog lived to seventeen—In dog years, the children told me, older than Rocky.

Jessica is in college.

Sam is a high school senior.

Joel Kerner is married and lives the life of a pious scholar. Some consider him a holy man.

On a sabbatical year in New York, I met and later married a woman who studies Talmud. We have daughters three and two.